LAKE EUROPA

A NEW CAPITAL FOR
A UNITED EUROPE

J. MARSHALL MILLER

1963
BOOKS INTERNATIONAL
134 Stockbridge Avenue, Alhambra, California 91801

What makes a city great? Huge piles of stone
Heaped heavenward? Vast multitudes who dwell
Within wide circling walls? . . .
True glory dwells where glorious deeds are done,
Where great men rise whose names athwart the dusk
Of misty centuries gleam like the sun! . . .
So may the city that I love be great
Till every stone shall be articulate.

William Dudley Foulke
1848-1935

Dedicated to those pioneers, who through the centuries have
given their lives and fortunes in the pursuit of truth and for
political and religious freedom,—and whose noble words and
deeds comprise a rich heritage inspiring us to live at peace
with our fellow man and in fear of Almighty God.

Printed in the United States of America
Library of Congress catalog card number: 62-21151

i

CONTENTS

PREFACE

It is not the purpose of this book to outline a "plan" for the physical development of a new city; rather, the objective is to set forth an idea, to propose the creation of a new capital for a rapidly uniting Europe—the City of Lake Europa.

The author is convinced that the idea of a new European capital is both valid and timely, a conviction based on the following facts:

COMMON MARKET PROVES WESTERN EUROPE CAN COOPERATE.

1) The proven success of the Common Market demonstrates that the countries of Europe can effectively cooperate, set common goals, and achieve those goals. It also seems to be a foregone conclusion that it is only a matter of time—and a relatively short time—before all of the countries of Western Europe will be members of one economic community.

EXISTING CITIES UNSUITABLE FOR NEW CAPITAL.

2) In spite of the war-damaged cities which are now rebuilt, practically every city of Western Europe is crowded and becoming more so. The street systems for the most part are obsolete with unbearable traffic congestion. Most of the structures are old and outmoded. Open areas are relatively few and parks inadequate for the expanding population. No existing city could possibly provide the vast areas needed for the countless buildings required for a new capital without destroying great portions of the existing physical structure of the community, and resulting in a relocation problem which would be beyond solution. In short, no existing European city is a reasonable, suitable, or proper location for a new capital. This conclusion holds true, especially, of the present capital cities.

3) It would be politically unrealistic to assume that the countries of Europe would look with favor on the idea of choosing an existing city wholly within any country for a European capital. This would be particularly so if the location proposed were an existing capital.

NEW CAPITAL DISTRICT POLITICALLY ADVISABLE.

4) History has demonstrated that most new capitals have been located as a compromise—usually the result of a struggle between two or more centers of population. The same philosophy of compromise would apply to the location of a new European capital. Anticipating the acceptance of a compromise location —in open country—it seems logical that any new capital district would be more acceptable if located at the junction of three or more countries, at a fairly central place which would be relatively accessible from most of the major areas of population. A study of the map of Europe quickly shows that there is only one location that meets these qualifications: the junction of the countries of France, Germany, and Luxembourg.

5) Administrative efficiency in any organization, public or private, demands the centralization of certain functions. The close physical proximity of the headquarters of many existing international organizations would minimize the waste of time and funds now expended in the participation of key personnel in inter-organization conferences. As greater cooperation between the peoples of Europe materializes, with the expansion of present organizations and the creation of new bodies, it is essential that headquarters of these numerous groups be centralized in some convenient location. A politically united Europe, irrespective of the type of governmental structure, would demand a new capital.

FUNCTIONAL CENTRALIZATION ESSENTIAL FOR ADMINISTRATIVE EFFICIENCY.

Based on these fundamental facts and logical conclusions, the site for the proposed capital would focus on the junction of France, Germany, and Luxembourg, in the valley of the Mosel River. The advantages of the site are outlined in Chapter 7.

The layout of the actual plan for the physical development of the capital and its metropolitan region could well be the subject of one or more international competitions, and could be sponsored by the Lake Europa Development Authority (LEDA), proposed in Chapter 7. This Authority could be created before the extent of the actual site is finally determined.

SUGGEST INTERNATIONAL COMPETITIONS FOR PLAN OF NEW CAPITAL.

The major concepts for the new capital are spelled out in Chapter 7 in sufficient detail to form the basis for the organization of a program for the design of the metropolis. Several sketches give clues to what the author has in mind for elements of the physical structure. It was thought wise not to develop this graphic presentation in detail. It is hoped that the combination of the sketches and the textual description will fire the imagination of the reader and in no way limit his own vision of the appearance of the new capital. The prime objective of the book is to try to convey the concept, need, and logic of a new capital for Europe. Once the idea is accepted, and a location determined, the details of development will follow.

The writer feels that the first six chapters form a firm foundation for the proposal. Chapter 8 indicates the possible application to other metropolitan areas, old or new, of some of the concepts outlined in Chapter 7. The four appendices record information which tends to substantiate some of the views expressed in the preceding text.

The concept of a new European capital was briefly outlined by the author on the 23rd of August, 1958, in his remarks at the opening session of the First International Seminar on Urban Renewal held in The Hague. In retrospect, the writer recalls that his fellow seminar participants thought the suggestion a

NEW CAPITAL PROPOSED IN 1958.

2

far-fetched and impossible idea. However, events of the past few years have clearly demonstrated that Europe is moving rapidly toward some form of unity, and the idea of a new capital is a concept which can no longer be considered impossible.

ACKNOWLEDGEMENTS.

Many individuals and professional friends on both sides of the Atlantic, have encouraged the development of the proposal as here set forth. Special thanks are due to Bob Frommes, Roger Krieps and Tony Krier of Luxembourg. Mr. Frommes gave much encouragement and supplied base maps of the region. Messrs. Krieps and Krier, with newspaper articles and photos, did much to promote the idea in Europe. For the many maps the author is deeply grateful to Astrid and Henry W. Stone, and for the superb color plates a special word of thanks is expressed to Robert E. Schwartz. A deep debt of gratitude is also due Dorothy Humphries, Phyllis Moehrle and Margaret Swan for checking the manuscript, editing, and proofing the galleys. For assisting in page composition, type selection, and final proofing I am grateful to Mabel Bigger and Robert V. Frey of The Bigger Press, Inc. Last, but far from least, my deepest appreciation goes to my wife, Helen. Without her constant encouragement, typing, editing, and proofing, this volume may never have come into existence. For the text, other than material quoted or reprinted, the author, of course, accepts full responsibility, including errors or omissions.

J. Marshall Miller
New York City
November 1962

—The choice is clear, not only for our leaders, but for every one of us: We choose between greatness — and oblivion. "Where there is no vision, the people perish." These words have an ominous, familiar ring. But reverse them and they become bright with hope and challenge. For history has demonstrated again that "Where there is vision, the people triumph!"
Arthur C. Clarke
1960

3

1

INTRODUCTION

Through the centuries, powerful personalities have emerged, and, by force of arms, have swept devastatingly back and forth across the face of Europe. With tyrannical and selfish philosophies, these would-be supermen have marshaled sufficient followers and resources under their crusading banners to venture forth in bloody conquest against all foes.

The torn breast of the European landscape records ghastly evidence of the recurring, insane savagery of man against man. Repeated inhuman forays have led not only to havoc, destruction, and death—but to continuing mistrust and hatred.

The European Neanderthal man hunted food and foe with club and axe in his daily struggle for survival. Through thousands of years, man has been making his way, step by step, over the dead bodies of his neighbors, from prehistoric barbarism to contemporary barbarism. Weapons have changed, but man's will has not.

Man's inborn desire to survive, his will to live, his animal nature to dominate, has always warped his mental outlook on life, and has driven him invariably toward the irrational and inhuman conviction that in order to survive he must kill, or be killed. Peace has ever been conceived as a state of pseudo relaxation, where one person or group is completely subjugated to another, usually by brute force. "Freedom" was the privilege of the victor—slavery, the lot of the vanquished.

Europe has witnessed recurring attempts to build empires, from Alexander the Great to Hitler. Without exception, these domains have emerged as a result of conquest by force, even though at times brute force was cloaked in the guise of religion.

A great question now arises. Since World War II, have Europeans, as individuals and as nations, conceived that peace is possible through cooperative unity, and without resorting to weapons of war? Can a new day be dawning wherein the peoples of Europe might live in harmony with their neighbors? Conflicting philosophies may never permit total agreement; but may we expect a period in which conflicting philosophies might co-exist without (and even with a high degree of intersectional cooperation) the constant fear that adherents of one self-centered philosophy will deliberately try to dominate those with different beliefs? While it would be naive to delude oneself

MAN'S WILL TO DOMINATE.

EUROPE UNITED MANY TIMES BY FORCE OF ARMS.

4

that peaceful co-existence is a logical next step, may we ever have faith that this is worth every human effort to achieve?

Throughout European history there have been endless treaties: military treaties, peace treaties, trade agreements, economic agreements, pacts for cooperative aggression, pacts for protection, pacts for cooperation against aggression.

A NEW VISION OF UNITY.

Since the last war, nations of the European community have entered into scores of agreements with the aim of achieving cooperation, international understanding, and mutual benefits. These documents literally have been symbols of harmony— positive indications of deliberate and constructive attempts to live at peace and to achieve common goals. Do these numerous symbols—now mostly economic, military, and cultural — foreshadow political unity in the not too distant future?

SURVIVAL DEMANDS UNITY.

While the Europeans are beginning to realize some of the advantages of economic cooperation, they might be driven to unite politically if they are to survive. As long as the Soviet Union adheres to its policy of world domination, by dividing and conquering, it is essential that the countries of Western Europe bind themselves together in whatever forms of unity and cooperation necessary to discourage any possible advances which the Russians may have in mind. History has proven that there is no greater force for uniting peoples than the presence of a common enemy. The peoples of Europe are beginning to realize that some form of union is not only desirable from the standpoint of providing a better life for all—but that union is the only logical alternative for maintaining life and freedom. While European unity may not result in the pattern of peace which all might desire, it may well hold back the tides of war.

The magic of belief: She was a peasant, unlettered and poor in a world of pomp and power. But Joan of Arc had faith. That faith was a candle in the dark, a fire that melted fear, transformed doubt into doing, defeat into victory. So much is possible with faith — strong, unswerving belief in a cause, an idea, an ideal . . . and in ourselves. So little is ever achieved without it.
Tennessee Gas
Transmission Company
Advertisement in
TIME Magazine
1962

2

HISTORICAL FORCES, DRIVES, AND

SYMBOLS OF EUROPEAN UNITY

(Alexander The Great to Hitler)

For several centuries prior to 1200 B.C., the Aegeans dominated the southeastern portion of what is now known as the continent of Europe. Their area of influence ranged from the shores of Asia Minor across the islands of the eastern Mediterranean and Aegean seas to the peninsulas of Greece and Italy and the island of Sicily.

Powerful sea-kings ruled both sea and land as despotic monarchs. Sumptuous palaces graced the hilly slopes of the island of Crete where the kings and their courts lived in luxury. The sea-going Cretans, with their handsome capital at Knossos, developed a high level of culture, particularly in arts and architecture. Along with the Cretan capital, the towns of Mycenae and Tiryns on the Greek mainland were famed abroad for their classic elegance. On the eastern shores of the Aegean, the city of Troy was rebuilt after repeated attempts by enemies to destroy it. Canals and sanitary sewer systems were not uncommon. Royal residences had sanitary facilities with elaborate shower baths which would compare favorably with the best bathrooms of today.

KNOSSOS CAPITAL OF CRETAN EMPIRE.

Worshiping the Greek Earth Mother, the Aegeans were sturdy, athletic folk, delighting in strenuous physical games. Even the Cretan maidens would rollick, unarmed and unprotected, with wild bulls in a Minoan version of a bull ring performance.

The Aegean civilization reached two recognizable crests: First, about 1800 B.C., and again about 1500 B.C. Knossos was destroyed, possibly by earthquake, about 1730 B.C. But from the ruins grew a new and more beautiful city with the renewed life and vigor which so often occurs after a catastrophe.

About 1450 B.C., barbaric tribes from the north (later known as Greeks) were attracted by the glamor of the Aegean cities and by the beauty of the Minoan maids. Slowly but steadily the early Greeks—the Dorians, Ionians, Eolians, and Aetolians —pushed south. Tiryns and Mycenae fell, then Knossos, and

GREEK CITIES SYMBOLS OF LOCAL SOVEREIGNTY.

Liberty . . . is best managed in a democratic city, and for this reason that is the only city in which a man of free spirit will care to live.
Plato
427-347 B. C.

ROME UNITES SOUTHEAST EUROPE.

finally, with the fall of Troy, the remaining Cretans were driven into Syria, scattered or destroyed.

The rugged freedom-loving Greeks resisted formal national political unity—preferring that autonomy be retained by the city. The Greek "city-states" were symbols of local sovereignty from before 1200 B.C. to the broader forced domination by Alexander the Great in the 4th Century B.C. The far-flung Macedonian Empire of Alexander was nourished and maintained by decisive military conquests. Although the aristocratic Greeks were united in arts and letters for several decades after Alexander, they failed to obtain the political unity necessary for national survival. It is little wonder then, as the Roman legions pressed south and east under the banner of the young and vigorous Roman Republic, founded in the 4th Century B.C., that the disunited Greeks failed to repulse the united Romans. By 300 B.C., Rome had completed the conquest of the entire Italian peninsula, and with the flush of victory looked for new lands to conquer.

By 100 B.C., Roman imperialism was fully developed, the Roman Senate had been established, Philip V of Greece had been defeated, Carthage had been destroyed, eight Roman provinces had been established under Roman law, and Rome emerged as the master of the western world. Roman political and social life, especially during the period between the fall of Carthage (251-240 B.C.) and the rise of Caesar (60 B.C.), and Caesarism, was, in fact, a primitive and clumsy form of "representative democracy" not unlike those presently in operation in the United States of America or in the British Empire. For the first time in history, Rome had demonstrated that political, social, and cultural unity was possible and workable under a form of representative "democratic" government based on a code of laws.[1]

For five centuries (c. 200 B.C. - c. 300 A.D.) Rome dominated the greater portion of Europe and the then known western world. Never before had there been such a widespread feeling of security. Roman magistrates, backed by Roman legions, were present throughout Rome's scattered provinces. The impact of Roman law and military force was tempered with the philosophy and the scholastic humanitarianism of the Greeks, and the influence of Grecian culture permeated the Roman Empire. However, Rome's legal codes in no way assured a moral or ethical code. Political intrigue was as prevalent then as it is today, if

---

[1]H. G. Wells, "The Outline of History" (Garden City, New York: Garden City Publishing Company, Inc., 1931), p. 445.

not more so. Many Romans were highly versed in the art of "politicking," with all the cunning, the good and the evil inherent in that term. In any far-flung empire there are always many important commercial, religious, and administrative centers. However, the Roman Empire had but one undisputed imperial capital—the City of Rome.

The decline and fall of the Roman Empire had many roots: internal emergence of tyranny and destruction of the Senate, softness of political and military leaders as a result of luxury and over-indulgence, infiltration of the Roman armies by anti-Roman Goths from the northern frontiers, and, last but far from least, the rapid spread of Christianity.[2] Never before had a religious philosophy spread so fast, drawn so many converts, made such an impact on the minds, hearts, and works of men. As the political unity of Rome lapsed, unity of action in the Early Christian Church manifested itself throughout the civilized world, bringing new hope to the lives of countless millions of men and women wearied by the insanity and brutality of tyrannical wars and bloodshed. Here was the vision of a new unity, a new concept of life which brought converts from all ranks of society—from the humblest slave to the imperial Emperor.

Although Constantine the Great, upon his ascension to the Roman throne in 306 A.D., restored authority to the Roman Senate, he is primarily known to have been instrumental in calling a halt officially to the persecution of the Christians. Constantine presided over the first general council of the Christian Church in Nicaea (near Constantinople) in 325 A.D., and the Emperor was baptized into the Christian faith upon his death bed. Perhaps the single, most noteworthy claim of originality to be recorded about this forceful leader was his manifest understanding of the need of some unifying moral force if the Empire were to hold together.[3]

Lacking the initial vision of Constantine, but adhering to his concepts for the need of unity, and well aware of the handwriting on the wall, the Roman Emperors immediately following Constantine, attempted to stamp out religious opposition and controversy by forceful political decree.

The Catholic dogmatism instigated by a combined man-controlled, religious-political leadership at this early date, stamped the heavy hand of anti-democratic (and actually anti-Christian) symbolism on the Roman Church. A review of the

DECLINE AND FALL OF ROME.

ROME BECOMES "CHRISTIAN."

EARLY CATHOLIC DOGMATISM AND CONTINUING TYRANNY.

[2]Edward Gibbon, "The Decline and Fall of the Roman Empire" (Great Books of the Western World, Volumes 40 and 41. Chicago: Encyclopaedia Britannica, Inc., 1952), Vol. I, pp. 179-255.
[3]Wells, *op. cit.*, p. 511.

8

records indicates that this heavy-handed, unyielding dogmatism still dominates the Roman Catholic Church in the mid-twentieth century, just as it has these past seventeen centuries. Is there actually much difference between a military or political tyrant and a religious tyrant? Is not tyranny, tyranny, irrespective of the cut or color of the garment worn by the tyrant? And worse, tyranny begets and demands brainwashing, and a brainwashed human, indoctrinated with misconceptions, loses his ability to think for himself—actually no longer a free man!

ROME DIVIDED INTO EAST AND WEST.

Rome, as a political entity, soon lost any semblance of unity. Political and religious discord reigned supreme. Politically and religiously, Rome split into two sections—the Western and Eastern Empires. For a few years, Theodosius the Great, held the two Empires together in a fragile unity. Upon his death in 395 A.D., the Empire was again divided, the City of Rome was captured and sacked.

The fifth century was a period of unrest, turmoil, disunity, and destruction throughout most of Western Europe. The Roman Empire had been shattered. Political and religious upheavals led directly to social, economic, and spiritual chaos. The Franks and Goths of Northern and Central Europe, together or separately, took most of Southern Europe by force.

EARLY RELIGIOUS-POLITICAL POWER STRUGGLES.

The sixth and seventh centuries witnessed a short period of domination of Southern and portions of Central Europe by the rulers of the later Roman or Byzantine Empire. This period was marked by political incompetence, internal strife and power struggles within the Catholic Church, military conflict with the Moslems on the South, and growing military strength of the Franks on the North.

About the year 700, vast portions of Southern Europe were united briefly under the Greco-Persian culture of the Moslem-Arabs. The Moslem advance was checked by a decisive victory at Tours, inflicted by the Frank, Charles Martel. This period also witnessed the early prominence of the British and Scandinavian countries.

Western Europe, during the eighth century, was a shattered civilization—without law, without administration; roads had been destroyed and education completely disorganized. Although there were many people with civilized ideas and traditions, it was an era of confusion, unpunished crimes, and universal insecurity. For physical protection, men linked themselves to stronger and more powerful individuals. This linkage between the protector and the subordinates developed rapidly into the feudal system.

Charles Martel divided his power between his two sons,

but one resigned and went into a monastery, leaving his brother Pippin, sole ruler of a vast, but disorganized portion of Western Europe. Pippin needed the blessing of the Pope to insure his "legal" crowning. The Pope, in need of a powerful supporter just at this time, decided in favor of Pippin, and the latter was crowned with the consent of the Pope in 751.

In 774, Charles, one of Pippin's two sons, became King of the growing realm of the Franks. This 'Charles' is known, historically, as Charles the Great (a self-conferred title), or Charlemagne.[4] The aggressive wars of Charlemagne were definitely religious conflicts. With fire and sword, the King carried the doctrine of the Roman Church through most of Europe. He drove the Moslems south into the Spanish peninsula as far as Barcelona. The pagan Saxons, continental English, and Scandinavian Vikings he drove into the sea. But his bloody attacks provoked bitter retaliations. The massacres and atrocities inflicted upon the 'unbelievers' by Charlemagne and his troops were anything but Christian. This persecution brought forth equally unchristian and inhuman counterattacks. Special delight was taken in burning nunneries and monasteries, and in the slaughter of their inmates.

Perhaps one positive result of the persecution of the Northmen (Vikings) was the exploration of the lands to the west. By the ninth century these hardy seamen had explored the shores of Greenland and had founded settlements on the mainland of North America. This new territory called "Vinland" was held but a short while. During the ninth century, the raids of the Northmen on their European neighbors developed into organized invasions. By 886, the Danes had conquered a good portion of England.[5]

Pope Leo III, being a hero worshiper of the conquering Charles, in a surprise ceremony in St. Peters in 800, crowned him Emperor of the West. Thus emerged the "Holy Roman Empire." Although the conquests of the Emperor kept him on the move most of the time, he usually returned to his home city of Aachen. Here he was born (742), and here he erected a magnificent palace, and here he was buried (814). Aachen, therefore, may well be considered the capital of the vast Carolingian Empire which encompassed the greater portion of Western Europe in the late 8th and 9th centuries.

Architecturally, there was a revival of Roman motifs throughout Charles' European Empire. These simple forms and

. . . the history of the world is nothing but the development of the idea of freedom.
Georg W. F. Hegel
1770-1831

---

[4]Henri Pirenne, "A History of Europe" (New York: University Books, 1955), pp. 80-86.
[5]Wells, *op. cit.*, pp. 647-648.

elements are classed as "Romanesque," the forerunner of early Gothic architecture.

Under Louis the Pious, son and successor of Charlemagne, the Empire fell apart.

The ninth and tenth centuries was an era of lawlessness, turmoil, and a continuing struggle for power. France and Germany were splintered into a mosaic of numberless small holdings, each held by a noble. This was a period of castle-building and construction of fortifications for individual properties, the romantic remains of which grace the countryside of Western Europe today. This was an age of "private wars."

Rome itself was in turmoil and deterioration, politically and religiously. With the decay of Charlemagne's Empire, the Pope was left without a protector, and was opposed by the unruly nobles, even in the City of Rome.

Two women of Rome, Theodora and Marozia, mother and daughter, were powerful and unscrupulous. Of the doings of these two, Wells writes: "Marozia seized and imprisoned Pope John X (928), who speedily died under her care. Her mother, Theodora, had been his mistress. Marozia subsequently made her illegitimate son the Pope, under the title of Pope John XI."[6]

The morals of Pope John XII were highly questionable, and his treachery resulted in his final degradation by the German Emperor Otto I.

With the crowning of Otto I in 962, a line of Saxon Emperors came into power and, during the next two centuries, the Holy Roman Empire had its heyday. This early period of the Middle Ages, however, was marked by almost continuous power struggles between Pope and Emperor for Empire control.

The imperial power of the Holy Roman Empire reached its zenith under the reign of Henry III in the mid-eleventh century. Although William of Normandy conquered England in 1066 and France was dominated by Philip I, the greater portion of the remainder of Central and Southern Europe—including most of Italy—was united under the German Emperors of the Holy Roman Empire.

The latter part of the 11th century also witnessed the sweep of the first crusades from Central Europe toward the Holy Land. The roots of the crusade movement were deep and complex. The motivating forces of these mass treks to the East ranged from high and religious goals to the baser concepts of hate and plunder. Even within the so-called "Christian" Roman Church was the cold and calculated scheme to subdue and replace the

[6]Wells, *op. cit.*, p. 658.

ERA OF "PRIVATE WARS" AND CASTLE BUILDING.

MOTIVATING FORCES FOR CRUSADES.

emperor-ruled Byzantine Church. This was simply a religious power struggle between the two principal religious forces which, combined, dominated vast portions of Europe and the Middle East. Ironically, these two groups both claimed that their rights and powers were based on the teachings of the same Christ.[1]

The crusades also gave a cloak of respectability to the freebooting instinct of the Normans who were tearing Italy to pieces. Reaching the Mediterranean, it was perhaps natural that the looting mobs turned their faces east toward new and richer fields to plunder. These complex forces in Europe were marshaled by the impassioned appeals of the ever-present propagandist who exaggerated the horrors and cruelties of the infidel. But once the forces of hate and conquest had been fanned into flame, the movement took on all of the uncontrollable and illogical aspects of a huge mob. The first waves of crusades might be likened to a flow of men toward a newly discovered gold field—a turbulent stream, heavy with the refuse of mankind—a flood bearing many sinners, but a few saints.

Irrespective of motives or achievements, the crusades united great numbers of Western Europeans. The crusades gave no real evidence of political or economic unity as we know it today; they were, rather, examples of social and religious unity which in reality might be interpreted as anti-social and anti-religious.

CRUSADES AS A UNIFYING FORCE.

The initial crusading force (1095-1096) was a "people's crusade," comprising two great leaderless mobs which moved slowly eastward, plundering as they traveled. The excesses of one of the crusading mobs provoked the Hungarians to massacre the entire horde. Another crusading group met a similar fate just east of the Bosporus.

The first organized crusade was summoned by Pope Urban II in 1095. Dominated by the Normans, these forces began moving from Western and Southern Europe in 1097. After many battles, Antioch was reached and captured. After a month's siege, Jerusalem was captured on 15 July 1099. The slaughter was terrible—the streets of the city ran red with the blood of the conquered. The First Crusade had ended.

FIRST CRUSADE.

The year 1147 saw the Second Crusade, with many French and Germans involved. One contingent headed east, another south through Spain to Portugal. These forces generated an opposing force which had its birth in Egypt. The result was a "counter crusade" and a series of engagements which, in fact, was a holy war. Egypt and Baghdad were reunited and Jerusa-

SECOND CRUSADE.

---

[1]The brief sketch of the crusades outlined in the following paragraph is based primarily on Wells, *op. cit.*, pp. 625-698.

THIRD CRUSADE.

lem retaken in 1187. This action provoked the Third Crusade (1189)—a grand and romantic affair, bristling with armored knights and courtly chivalry. However, Jerusalem was not taken. The Roman and Greek Churches were declared to be reunited, but this "unity" was short-lived.

"CHILDREN'S CRUSADE."

The Fourth Crusade, starting in Italy in 1202, took Constantinople. One of the paramount blots on the record of the Roman Church was the encouragement in 1212 of the "Children's Crusade." The insanity of this movement, affecting thousands of children in France, Germany, and Switzerland, resulted in shiploads of deluded and innocent children being sold into slavery in Egypt, and other hundreds perishing in their march through Italy. The inhumanity of Pope Innocent III was obvious when he tried to capitalize on the disaster of the Children's Crusade to generate enthusiasm for a Fifth Crusade.

SIXTH CRUSADE.

A Sixth Crusade bordered on absurdity. In a struggle for political power in Italy, between Pope Gregory IX and the German Emperor Frederick II, the Pope demanded that the Emperor hold to a stupid vow. Frederick II remained evasive, and the Pope excommunicated him, proclaimed a crusade against him, and invaded the Emperor's Italian domains. Frederick sailed for the Holy Land, entered into a trade agreement with the Sultan of Egypt, returned to Italy, consolidated his holdings there, and forced the Pope to absolve him from his excommunication.

SEVENTH CRUSADE.

The Seventh Crusade, led by Louis IX, King of France, ended in his imprisonment. Later recaptured, he returned to his home country. The Eighth, and last Crusade, led by this same Louis IX against Tunis, ended in failure and in the death of its leader by fever.

The emotion and unifying influence of the crusades had passed. These adventures were basically outward expressions of struggles for power—the Roman Church against the Greek Church; the so-called "Christian" West against the Moslem East; the Pope against the rebellious rulers of Europe, and vice versa.

EUROPE CONTINUES IN TURMOIL DURING LATTER MIDDLE AGES.

For several centuries following the crusades, Europe was once again splintered—socially, politically and religiously. During the latter years of the Middle Ages (1250-1450), the lives of many Europeans were dominated religiously by the Roman Church. Tangible expressions of this Catholic influence are the hundreds of Gothic churches which still tower over many of the European towns and cities. But religious unrest prevailed. The dogmas, corruption, and political maneuvering of the Roman Church caused much unrest and serious reflection, even among the would-be devout. Reform was inevitable.

Among many disasters which befell the peoples of Europe during this period was the Great Plague, or Black Death of 1348-1349. It is estimated that about 25 million persons died. In some areas as high as two-thirds to three-fourths of the population were fatally stricken. Cities were especially hard hit, with many of the communities of Western Europe losing half of their inhabitants.

Another historical and disastrous event during these times was the split in the Roman Church known as the Great Schism. This intra-church break occurred in 1378 when two popes were reigning in Western Europe, both having considerable political support. Each Pope excommunicated and cursed adherents of his rival. During the period 1378-1417, the Roman Catholic Church again demonstrated how far it had ventured from the teachings of Christ.

ROMAN CATHOLIC CHURCH SPLIT BY THE GREAT SCHISM.

In 1464, George Podiebrad, a Czech nobleman, and King of Bohemia, advanced a plan intended to bring peace to Europe and to enable the Christian nations to unite against the invading Turks. Podiebrad knew from bitter experience the perils of disunity. His plan was interesting because it was the first to include concrete details. Inasmuch as Podiebrad's plan undermined some of the power of the Roman Church, the Papacy excommunicated him and set the Catholic King of Hungary against his country. Podiebrad barely managed to maintain his people's independence in the face of Catholic aggression.[8]

In the early 16th century, Charles V of Spain, grandson of Emperor Maximilian, attempted to reestablish the Holy Roman Empire. In June 1519, by a vast amount of bribery, Charles was elected German Emperor. Backed by the Roman Church, the new Emperor set forth to consolidate his Empire.[9] But Northern Germany was already in the throes of reformation and would bow neither to the Church nor to the new Catholic Emperor. Many years of conflict ensued.[10]

Charles soon came face to face with Martin Luther, and their conflicting views on the Church at once erupted. Luther sparked the Reformation, Charles gave birth to the Counter Reformation. The subsequent revolts embraced more bloody conflicts. As with many revolutionary movements, mobs got out

MARTIN LUTHER AND THE REFORMATION.

---

[8]Andrew and Frances Boyd, "Western Union: A Study of the Trend Toward European Unity" (Washington D.C.: Public Affairs Press, 1949), pp. 27-28.

[9]Wells, *op. cit.*, p. 794.

[10]Gertrude von Schwarzenfeld, "Charles V, Father of Europe" (Chicago: Henry Regnery Company, 1957), pp. 50-79.

of hand. Confused revolt was everywhere. Over continuous objections from Spanish royalty, Charles demanded Spanish financial support for his Central and Southern European campaigns. Even with reluctant home support the tide of reform and revolt could not be stemmed. Finally, frustrated and bewildered, his dreams of a vast empire evaporated, at the age of 57, Charles withdrew from the world of reality into the protection and solitude of a Spanish monastery.[11]

One of the greatest forces which swept over Northern Europe in the 16th and 17th centuries was the Reformation—a thrust both for unity and disunity. While the power of this force was directed against the Roman Catholic Church, and the widespread corruption in which the Church indulged, or which it shielded, it was at the same time a force which was to unite the peoples of Northern Europe into a strong Protestant Movement which thrived and expanded under persecution by the Catholic Church, and by reason of the unfolding of the truths of the Bible. To try to prevent the breaking away from the power of the Roman Church, the Catholic Hierarchy condoned and advocated the institution of inhuman torture commonly known as the "Inquisition."[12]

THE INQUISITION.

Religious unrest was mounting among the devout peoples of Central and Northern Germany: an unrest and growing dissatisfaction with the practices of the Roman Church, agitated by commercialization of the practice of selling indulgences, claiming that cash payments to the Church representatives would release souls from purgatory, and that a living person could even be absolved from his worldly sins, irrespective of their nature. The growing distaste for such false claims was further magnified by the knowledge that most of the hard-earned monies required for these indulgences was sent off to Rome to pile up unnecessary wealth for an already wealthy, lavish, and corrupt papacy.[13]

These practices were openly critized by several of the German preachers. Martin Luther was one of the leaders in this criticism of the Church.[14] Angered by a fresh drive for indulgences in 1517, Luther set down in writing his beliefs concerning the situation and nailed a printed copy of his ninety-five theses

---

[11]*Ibid.*, pp. 80-86.

[12]See Appendix B for "A Brief Sketch of the Inquisition - 4th to 20th Century."

[13]Henry Charles Lea, "A History of the Inquisition of the Middle Ages" (New York: Russell & Russell, 1958, in three volumes), Vol. I, pp. 41-47.

[14]J. H. Merle D'Aubigné, "The Life and Times of Martin Luther" (Chicago: Moody Press, 1958), 559 pp.

to the door of his own church, the Castle Church in Wittenberg.[15] Copies in Latin were sent to several German church leaders and scholars. His intention was to initiate debate and definition. However, copies soon appeared in German and before long Luther's Theses became the talk of Germany. A copy shortly reached Rome. On April 18, 1521, before Emperor Charles V at the Diet of Worms, Luther was asked, "Do you or do you not repudiate your books and the errors which they contain?" Luther replied, ". . . Unless I am convicted by Scripture and plain reason—I do not accept the authority of popes and councils, for they have contradicted each other—my conscience is captive to the Word of God. I cannot and I will not recant anything, for to go against conscience is neither right nor safe. Here I stand, I cannot do otherwise. God help me. Amen." The Diet condemned Luther of heresy.[16] But the die had been cast. The period of the Reformation had already begun.[17]

Throughout Western Europe the new spirit of revolt against Roman Catholicism spread like wildfire. Noblemen joined devout Protestants in their drive for freedom from both the religious rule of the Church and from the political rule of Catholic-minded rulers. While the rebellion was widespread, it reached its bloodiest height in the Low Countries. The Netherlands, having been for some time under the political jurisdiction of the devout Catholic King of Spain, sought freedom from both political and religious tyranny. Philip, King of Spain, and his local henchman, Alva, vowed not to leave a single unbeliever alive. But Alva was repulsed and, after numerous struggles for the better part of a century, a semblance of independence was finally achieved for much of Northwestern Europe by the Treaty of Westphalia in 1648.

The mid-seventeenth century witnessed two interesting but unsuccessful experiments in European groupings. In 1658, Philip von Schoenberg, Archbishop of Mainz, persuaded the small Rhenish states to form a federation to settle their disputes by peaceful conciliation. Unfortunately, the combined strength of the Rhenish states was no match for that of France, and the confederation died an early death.

A more grandiose scheme was proposed in the "Grand Design of Henry IV." This volume first published in France in 1638 was enlarged in 1662. Actually, the brain child of Henry IV's minister, Maximilian de Bethune, Duc de Sully, the "design"

MARTIN LUTHER DEFIES THE ROMAN CHURCH AND CHARLES V.

PROTESTANT REVOLT UNITES NORTHERN EUROPE.

EARLY ATTEMPTS AT EUROPEAN UNITY.

SULLY'S PLAN FOR UNITY.

[15]Roland H. Bainton, "Here I Stand" (New York: Abingdon Press, 1950), pp. 79-83.
[16]*Ibid.*, pp. 181-190.
[17]D'Aubigné, *op. cit.*, pp. 540-546.

recommended a revision of the entire political structure of the Continent. Fifteen political units were suggested with consideration given to religious and military details. Sully's plan was never given serious consideration because it was evident that he had given far too much importance to the "benefits" which would accrue from French domination in the scheme.[18]

Another plan for European unity was set forth in considerable detail in 1693 by William Penn, the founder of Pennsylvania. In 1710, John Bellers, another Quaker, published still a different suggestion under the title "Some Reasons for a European State Proposed to the Powers of Europe." Bellers looked forward to the eventual uniting of all Europe in one state.

Only two years later, Charles Irenee Castel, Abbé de Saint-Pierre, an experienced diplomat, published his plan for "Perpetual Peace in Europe." His proposal met with considerable favor in diplomatic circles and the details of his proposed administrative setup appeared to be logical. Being both a realist and a philosopher, Castel admitted that he did not look forward to an early fulfillment of his project, stating that "Great institutions are only gradually made."[19]

Paralleling the Reformation, and a vivid expression of the same general movement, was the emergence of the "Renaissance." Just as there was a sustained drive for an effective break with the spiritual elements associated with the Roman Church, so there was a drive to break with the cultural elements associated with the Church-dominated Gothic Middle Ages. The Renaissance, or "rebirth" of interest in pre-Gothic forms and forces, initiated a vast building boom which resulted in hundreds of classic-inspired palaces, town houses and civic structures. The spirit of the Renaissance finally swept through the hard core of the Catholic Church. Out of this period came the design forms which still dominate most of the cities of Western Europe as well as the Americas. The cities of Rome, Florence, Munich, Paris, London, and Washington, are but a few of the hundreds of communities which are primarily Renaissance in design. As a cultural and artistic force, the Renaissance may well be classed as a "force for unity." Certainly it called forth a desire and drive for culture and artistic unity on a vast international scale, the like of which has not been seen before or since.

By the mid-19th century, the so-called "purer" forms of Renaissance design had already degenerated into the hodge-

---

[18]Boyd, *op. cit.*, pp. 28-29.
[19]Boyd, *op. cit.*, pp. 30-32.

podge of architecture known as "eclectic." Due to a universal dearth of creative ability for the last several centuries, this "bastard architecture" (a degenerate form of the Renaissance which, of itself, was mostly illegitimate) has blighted the human environment with architectural monstrosities. Unfortunately too, most of these structures are still standing.

Historically, of course, these degenerate art forms are but an evidence of a degenerate social order—a period in history lacking in great creative minds, of men strong enough to venture forth against the tide. Fortunately, during the last half century, a few creative individuals have emerged and their design philosophies are now beginning to be rather widely accepted. Leaders in this new movement include such men as Patrick Geddes, Louis Sullivan, the late Frank Lloyd Wright, Walter Gropius, Mies van der Rohe, Richard Neutra. Newcomers which may be considered to belong to this same contemporary school of creative design are Raphael Soriano, Welton Becket, Victor Gruen, Edward Stone, Robert Schwartz, and many others. The mental design barriers of the Renaissance and eclecticism have been pierced, and we may look to the emergence of new creative and dynamic forms which will give an entirely new pattern to our cities.

DEGENERATE ART FORMS REFLECT DEGENERATE SOCIETY.

But let us note other unifying forces at play in Western Europe since the early years of the Renaissance. The greater portion of the 17th and 18th centuries might be called the period of "Grand Monarchies" in Western Europe. Despite numerous military conflicts between nations, there was a common and widespread desire to aspire to a higher level of "cultural aristocracy." During this period Louis XIV of France was perhaps the dominant figure—the one who set the "aristocratic fashion" of the day. Other European monarchs did their best to imitate the French ruler from copying the Palace of Versailles, to the costumes, music, literature, and general lack of morality and virtue.

Although the rulers and their courts in France, Spain, and Italy, gave lip service to the Roman Catholic Church, and persecuted the growing number of zealous Protestants, their actions could hardly be called "Christian." Public life in France, and in most of Western and Southern Europe, was dominated during this long period by fickle and unscrupulous rulers, by court "ladies" of questionable virtue, and by an irreligious and parasitic noble class which sowed the seeds of its own downfall. Revolution was inevitable.

FRENCH REVOLUTION.

In the mid-18th century, the famous French philosopher, Jean-Jacques Rousseau, set forth a revised version of Saint-

18

ROUSSEAU REVIVES CASTEL PLAN FOR EUROPEAN UNITY.

NAPOLEON BONAPARTE TRIES TO UNIFY EUROPE.

Pierre's project.[20] Between 1750 and 1800, no less than twenty-three separate plans for preserving the peace of Europe were published in various countries. The so-called Age of Reason naturally gave birth to many such philosophical concepts. Most of these proposals had little effect on the minds of men.[21]

The nineteenth century witnessed three eras in which considerable areas of Europe approached a form of unity. The first of these three periods had a dual foundation. On the one hand, the Reign of Terror in France (1793-94) resulted in the execution of thousands of individuals, including most of the so-called nobility. This left the country destitute of trained, or recognized, leadership. On the other hand, from this political chaos, emerged a small, but powerful, military figure—Napoleon I. Born in 1769, young Bonaparte was trained at military schools and took some part in the French revolutionary action in Paris, Corsica, and Marseilles in 1792. After a series of brilliant but hectic military engagements in Italy, Austria, and Egypt, he returned to Paris, and on November 9, 1799, overthrew the Directory, the revolutionary ruling committee of the country. He set up a "Consulate" with himself as the first Consul. After another series of outstanding, but dictatorial, interior political moves, he was crowned Emperor (of France) on December 2, 1804, and assumed the title "King of Italy" the following year.[22]

During the next ten years (1805-15) by spectacular military campaigns, the forces of Napoleon defeated one army after another. In 1806 he dissolved the remnants of the Holy Roman Empire. He managed to defeat numerous coalitions which came forward to oppose him. His lust for conquest led him to invade Russia in 1812. After reaching Moscow, his fortunes began to turn against him. In retreat his army suffered greatly. After his surviving troops were defeated at Leipsig in 1813, he withdrew to France and was forced to abdicate in April 1814. However, he returned to Paris, and to military command the following year, only to be defeated finally at Waterloo on June 18 of the same year.

The second great era of harmony in Europe during the 19th century emerged from the confusion left in the wake of the

---

[20]In 1712, Charles Irenee Castel, Abbé de Saint-Pierre, an experienced French diplomat, published his plan for "Perpetual Peace in Europe." Saint-Pierre proposed a permanent Senate of Peace, continuously in session, with a rather elaborate organizational structure. The President of the Senate would be titled the "Prince of Peace." This plan, also known as the "Grand Alliance," became widely known, but never was seriously considered.

[21]Boyd *op. cit.*, pp. 32-33.

[22]William S. Roeder, Editors, "Dictionary of European History (New York: Philosophical Library, 1954), pp. 194-195.

retreats and defeats of Napoleon. Perhaps it was only natural that those who opposed the French Emperor would cast about for a basis for continuing friendly relations. The monarchs of Russia, Austria, and Prussia labored under the delusion that in defeating Napoleon, they had quieted, if not conquered, the revolutionary forces upon the waves of which Napoleon had ridden to conquest. These monarchs formed a somewhat formal, but loose, coalition known as the Holy Alliance. This soon gave place to a more realistic league of nations, the Concert of Europe.[23] In 1818 France joined this league, and in 1822 Britain withdrew from it. For forty years the concert of nations maintained an uneasy peace. However, the aromatic perfume of revolution still lingered to excite the senses of those who felt oppressed by any form of monarchy.

THE HOLY ALLIANCE AND THE CONCERT OF EUROPE.

The third era of unity involved less territory, but the bonds of unity were stronger. As a result of joint action during the Franco-Prussian War (1870-71), the North German Confederation and the four South German States united on January 18, 1871, and King William of Prussia was proclaimed German Emperor. The union of the Germanic peoples of Central Europe, further strengthened by the Treaty of Frankfurt (May 10, 1871), laid the foundations of a strong resurgence of German nationalism and of a large nation with vast power—economically, politically, and militarily.[24] Under a Prussianized Germany, the heights and depths of supernationalism were one day to reap their reward—the devastation of its neighbors and its own eventual doom. Through the centuries, these have always been the fruits of ultra-nationalism. In one real sense, collective selfishness and pride are the degrading earmarks of undisciplined nationalism. Whether espoused by an individual or a nation these traits are but the vehicles to downfall.

GERMANIC PEOPLES UNIFY UNDER PRUSSIAN LEADERSHIP.

The philosophy of the new Germany was that labor was a national asset, and that the workers of the nation should be given every consideration from social legislation to a voice in government. The cementing of grass-roots support, and the advancement of the common man, were achieved through educating and organizing German citizens at all levels to develop and strengthen the cultural and scientific resources of a new Germany.

Unfortunately for Germany, for Europe, and for the world, the Prussian-bred emperors of the nation had vast imperialistic dreams which they were bent on carrying out. Unfortunately too,

GERMAN NATIONALISM LEADS TO DOWNFALL.

[23]Wells, *op. cit.*, pp. 949-950.
[24]Geoffrey Bruun, "Nineteenth Century European Civilization: 1815-1914" (New York: Galaxy Book, Oxford University Press, 1960), pp. 121-195.

power begets power, victory whets the appetite for further conquest. Power, and the lust for it, burned deep within the breasts of the German kaisers. The lust for power, as with all human lust, results in catastrophe. Dangerous and hazardous as a power drive is, once it gains momentum there seems to be no rational, face-saving method of applying brakes. Picking up ambitious supporters and additional fuel as it surges ahead, the drive generally rushes headlong into disaster. The devil is usually the victor.

Western Europe in the 20th century has witnessed three attempts to unite: the first two by military force; the third by a series of international agreements—mostly economic.

The first of the present century unification drives had its roots in the Franco-Prussian War of 1870-71. The greed of Germany in 1871 (Treaty of Frankfurt) made France her inveterate enemy. The expanding economic strength of Germany, in the last decades of the 19th century and the first decade of this century, nurtured a growing desire in the minds of the German kaisers to flex the strengthening political and military muscles of the nation which developed side-by-side with economic expansion. When one has enemies (and Germany had them to the East and to the West), and if one has been trained to fight—conflict is inevitable and natural. The only thing needed was an excuse to attack a possible adversary, and try to achieve a victory.

FIRST WORLD WAR.

The excuse materialized on June 28, 1914, with the assassination of Archduke Francis Ferdinand, heir to the Austrian Empire. The German Emperor accused Serbia of instigating the murder. Charges and countercharges were flung among many of the European countries during the month of July. On July the 30th, Russia mobilized her army, and on August the 1st, Germany declared war on her. The next day German troops crossed into French territory: World War I was under way.

The War generated a two-fold unity. On the offensive were Germany and her allies, Austria and Hungary, with the support of Bulgaria, Turkey, and the Ottoman Empire of the Middle East. On the defensive were Russia, France, Britain, Italy, Portugal, and the United States, along with numerous supporters. The war period produced a military unity of action and counteraction rather than political or territorial unity. By the time of the armistice on November the 11th, 1918, the conflict had left Europe exhausted. More than 30,000,000 people had been killed or had died of hardship. Physical resources had been wasted or plundered. As with most wars, all sides lost.

The agony which Europe suffered in 1914-1918 stimulated

efforts to prevent the recurrence of such conflicts. Vigorous international effort was devoted to the creation of a League of Nations. While its membership would include countries outside of Europe, there was the underlying belief that if the European quarrels could be brought under control (perhaps with the help of nations on other continents), both Europe and the world would reap the benefits. But, as Sir Winston Churchill later remarked, "The League of Nations did not fail because of its principles or conceptions. It failed because these principles were deserted by those states who brought it into being."[25]

But the memories and devastation of war are soon forgotten. And the lust for power rears its ugly head in every generation.

The scars of the First World War had not yet healed when there arose in Southern Germany, a semi-military organization under the leadership of Adolf Hitler. He soon won the support of many large industrialists, reorganized his political party (the German National Socialists), stressed anti-Semitism, anti-Marxism, and extreme nationalism. In 1933 Hitler was appointed Chancellor, and by exploiting the Reichstag fire (February 1933), he gained absolute control of the country. During the ensuing five years, he rearmed Germany, formed the Berlin-Rome Axis, annexed Austria, secured the Sudetenlands of Czechoslovakia, won Bohemia and Moravia, and seized Memel from Lithuania. Upon Poland's refusal to surrender the City of Danzig, Hitler attacked Poland (September 1939), thus unleashing the Second World War.[26]

Once again by force of arms, most of Europe fell under one ruler, but only for the duration of the war. During the early years of the conflict, Hitler's armies rolled over Poland, Denmark, Norway, Luxembourg, Holland, Belgium, France, Roumania, Yugoslavia, and Greece. His forces penetrated deep into Russia and across North Africa. In order to stabilize the Berlin-Rome Axis, Nazi troops occupied most of Italy. However, in 1942, the tide of victory began to turn. First in North Africa (at El Alamein in October), and then in Russia (at Stalingrad in November). In July 1943, the Western Allies landed in Sicily and Italy. The beachhead established by the allied troops in Normandy on June 6, 1944 (D-Day) was a major turning-point in the war. By the end of that first long day of invasion (the Longest Day), most of the Nazi military leaders realized that the dreams of Nazi conquest were rapidly turning into night-

LEAGUE OF NATIONS FAILS.

THE RISE AND FALL OF HITLER.

---

[25]Boyd, *op. cit.*, pp. 34-35.
[26]Roeder, *op. cit.*, pp. 134-135.

A NEW ERA OF EUROPEAN UNITY.

mares. The cracks in a united Europe under Hitler were widening rapidly. The collapse of Hitlerism was a certainty—it was now only a question of time. The end of the war in Europe came on May 7, 1945 (V-E Day). Hitler is alleged to have taken his own life on May 1.

The third era of unity in Europe in the twentieth century is now under way and appears to be gaining momentum and support. Actually, this era started in 1923 with the publication of a book entitled PAN-EUROPE by Count Coudenhove-Kalergi.[27] But this new era of European unity is the subject of the next chapter.

---

[27]Richard N. Coudenhove-Kalergi, "Pan-Europe" (New York: Alfred A. Knopf, 1926), 215 pp.

The world has become too small for physical, economic or political isolationism. The polarization of forces dueling for supremacy has gone too far to permit the survival of an island of humanism in a sea of dehumanized totalitarianism. No single nation can survive unless the civilization of which it is a part survives.

David Sarnoff
1960

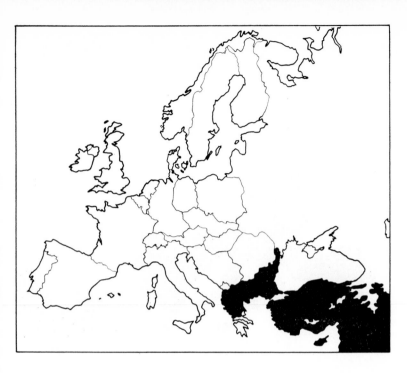

335-324 B.C.
Alexander the Great

The Campaigns and Empire of Alexander the Great extended from the Danube River in South-eastern Europe to beyond the Indus River in India.

150 B.C. Early Roman Power

The early Roman emperors consolidated their holdings in Southern Europe, Asia Minor, and along the Northern coast of Africa.

24

98 A.D.   Trajan

Under the rule of Trajan the Roman Empire reached its maximum extent. Most of Western, Central, and Southern Europe were united with the capital at Rome.

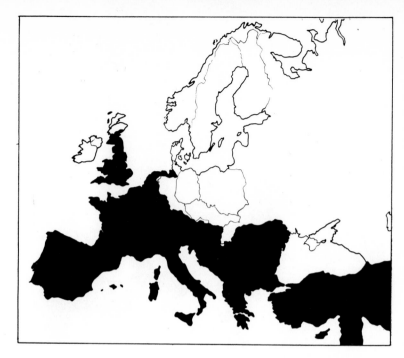

180 A.D.   Roman Empire under Marcus Aurelius

Rome continues to rule most of Western and Southern Europe, as well as the Eastern Mediterranean territories and the Northern coast of Africa.

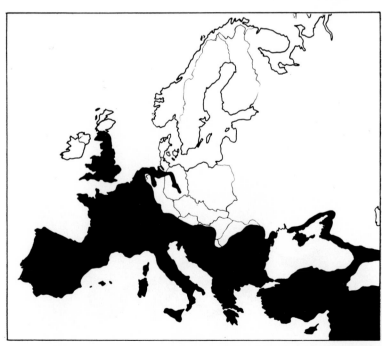

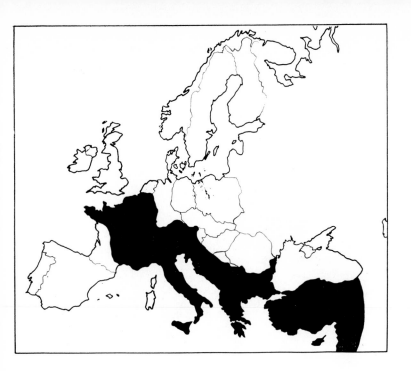

450 A.D. Rome declines

The rapid spread of Christianity, invasions from the North and West, internal decay, the splitting of the Empire into two sections with two capitals, combined to spell the rapid decline and fall of Rome.

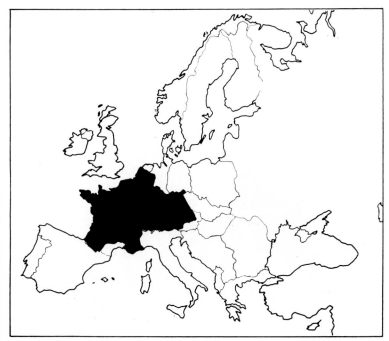

600 A.D. Franks under King Clovis

The Franks conquer portions of Western and Central Europe.

26

732 A.D. Charles Martel

The Frankish dominion in the time of Charles Martel.

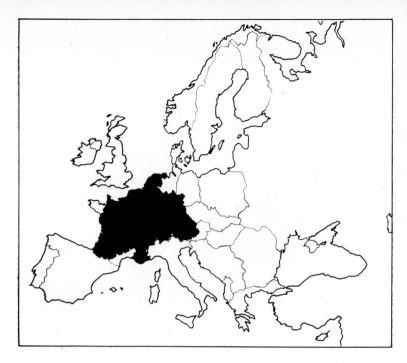

814 A.D. Charlemagne

By a series of religious wars Charles the Great united extensive areas of Western Europe forming the "Holy Roman Empire." The capital of the Carolingian Empire was Aachen.

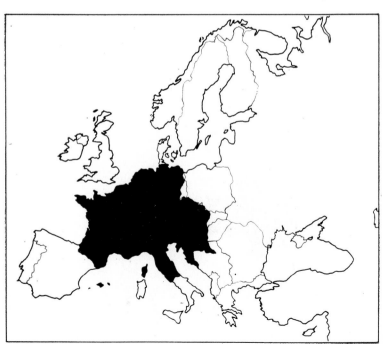

27

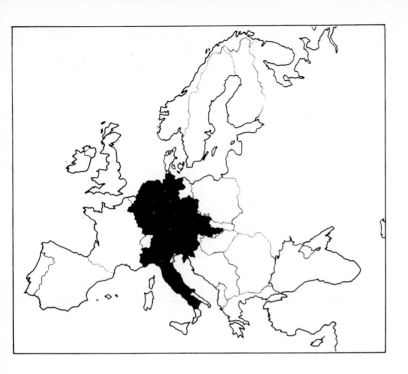

955 A. D. Otto the Great

Otto I (called the Great) was King of Germany and the Holy Roman Empire. His coronation in 962 revived the empire of Charlemagne.

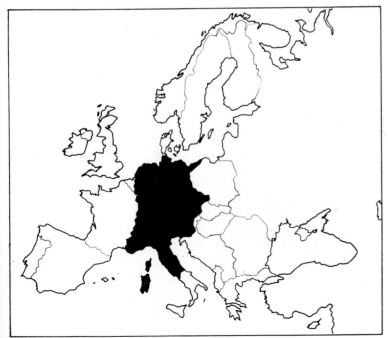

1190 A. D. The Holy Roman Empire

The German royal families of Hohenstaufens and Habsburgs succeeded in uniting Central Europe, including the Northern half of Italy.

1520 A. D.   Charles V

As King of Spain and Holy Roman Emperor, Charles V engaged in a series of "holy" wars with his neighbors. It was Charles V who called Martin Luther before the "diet" at Worms. Their conflicting views led to widespread revolt and the Reformation.

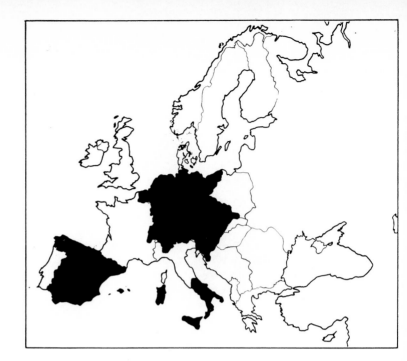

1812 A. D.   Napoleon

By a series of brilliant military campaigns, Napoleon I (Napoleon Bonaparte) unified most of Central and Western Europe. With Paris as his capital, his empire extended from Gibraltar to the Baltic. His forced retreat from Moscow in 1812 was soon followed by his final defeat at Waterloo.

1942 A.D. Hitler

The far-reaching conquests of Hitler during World War II. Berlin was the undisputed capital of the Nazi Empire.

. . . since wars begin in the minds of men, it is in the minds of men that the defences of peace must be constructed. . . .
    Unesco Constitution
    1945

3

CONTEMPORARY FORCES, DRIVES, AND

SYMBOLS OF EUROPEAN UNITY

(Since World War II)

NEW FOUNDATIONS FOR EUROPEAN UNITY.

The 1958-59 Yearbook of International Organizations[1] lists 1209 organizations, all of international character, the vast majority of which are wholly or mostly European. Europe may easily lay claim to being the most highly organized area on the earth, compared to any other land area of similar dimensions. One obvious reason — it got an early start.

However, in checking the dates of the founding of these hundreds of organizations, it is noted that the overwhelming majority have been established since the end of World War II. The horrors of that conflict, and the resulting devastation, seemed to instill in millions of Europeans the desire to try to cooperate rather than quarrel with their neighbors. Most Europeans finally realize that in any war everybody loses. Since V-E Day (7 May 1945), the peoples of Europe, if not their governments, have demonstrated that they seek to join with their fellow Europeans (of all nationalities) to face and try to solve common European problems — social, cultural, technical, professional, legal, and economic. At this date, the heads of several of the major European nations are constructively exploring avenues for greater political cooperation — perhaps some form of political unity.

The drives for postwar international cooperation in given areas have often been sparked by outstanding individuals, often by a leader in governmental, economic, or cultural circles. In most cases, these individuals have long been known for their desire to achieve international understanding and cooperation.

CONTEMPORARY FORCES FOR EUROPEAN UNITY.

The international organizations involving the cooperation of the peoples or governments of two or more European countries may be grouped into three major categories:[2] 1) the institutions of the European Community; 2) other intergovernmental organizations; and 3) international non-governmental

[1] "Yearbook of International Organizations," 7th Edition, 1958-59 (Brussels: Union of International Associations, 1958), 1269 pp.
[2] These are the groupings used by the Union of International Associations.

organizations.[3]

The first institution of the European Community group, and one of the largest, most powerful, and successful of all European international bodies, is the European Coal and Steel Community (ECSC). Proposed by Mr. Robert Schuman in 1950, it was officially established on the 25th of August, 1952.[4]

At the Messina Conference in June, 1955, resolutions were adopted in favor of European integration in certain given areas — the common market, the joint development of the major transport arteries, traditional sources of power, and atomic energy. Of the four projects proposed, two have already been inaugurated: the Common Market, and Euratom.[5] With the inauguration of the Eurailpass in 1959, the first step was taken for the integration of passenger transport. Several of the European airlines are presently considering the establishment of Air Union.

MESSINA CONFERENCE SPARKS EUROPEAN INTEGRATION.

The other institutions of the European Community are: European Economic Community (EEC), established 1 January 1958; Euratom, established 1 January 1958; European Parliamentary Assembly, with its first meeting 19-21 March 1958,[6] Court of Justice, established 25 March 1957; Economic and Social Committee, established 1 January 1958; European Investments Bank, established 25 March 1957. Two of these organizations have headquarters in the City of Luxembourg, four in Brussels.

The aims of the European Community organizations are primarily economic. However, in the day-to-day operations of these institutions, there is considerable involvement in the realms of politics, culture, health, welfare, etc. The organizations may be classed as semi-intergovernmental institutions of an extra-governmental character.

The second group of international organizations in Europe—all intergovernmental—takes on more of a political-economic-service-regulatory character.

One significant and active institution in this second group is the Council of Europe (CE). With the governments of fifteen European countries participating, and with headquarters in Strasbourg, France, it has a paid staff of several hundred employees which serves the Consultative Assembly of the Council, and a wide range of standing and general committees. The aims of this strong European international group are also significant:

COUNCIL OF EUROPE.

---

[3]See Appendix A.
[4]"Yearbook of International Organizations," p. 93.
[5]*Ibid.*, p. 92.
[6]*Ibid.*, p. 100.

to achieve a greater unity between its members for the purpose of safeguarding and realizing the ideals and principles which are their common heritage, and to facilitate their economic and social progress.[7]

Most problems of international transport come under the jurisdiction of one or two organizations: European Company for the Financing of Railway Rolling Stock (EUROFIMA); or the European Conference of Ministers of Transport (ECMT). In general, the aims of both organizations look toward the most rational use and development of European transportation.[8]

BENELUX ESTABLISHED.

The first steps toward closer economic ties between the three Benelux countries (Belgium, Netherlands, Luxembourg) were taken as early as 1944.[9] The ties were more firmly knit with the establishment of the inter-Parliamentary Consultative Council of Benelux in 1955, and by creating the Benelux Economic Union in 1958. These three organizations (the first non-governmental; the latter two, inter-governmental) have gone far in establishing sound economic ties between these three countries of Western Europe.

SIGNIFICANCE OF OECD.

Perhaps the key international economic institution of Western Europe is the Organization for Economic Cooperation and Development (OECD). It is an intergovernmental body with a staff of more than 800, which aims to coordinate all economic and financial measures between the eighteen member governments. This institution was first established in 1948 as the Organization for European Economic Cooperation (OEEC) and reorganized in 1961. Its headquarters are in Paris.

WESTERN EUROPEAN UNION ESTABLISHED.

One of the most outstanding intergovernmental organizations, advocating progressive integration and unity in Europe on all fronts, is the Western European Union. It was established on 6 May 1955, and has headquarters in London with a staff of over 100. Seven European governments (Belgium, France, German Federal Republic, Italy, Luxembourg, Netherlands, UK), are actively participating in promoting the unifying aims of this organization.

The Union of International Organizations groups the hundreds of international non-governmental organizations into eighteen categories—from "Bibliography, Documentation, and Press" to "Sport and Recreation."[10] Of the eighteen sub-groups, several have particularly large numbers of international organizations. These more extensive categories include: Religion and

[7]*Ibid.*, p. 123.
[8]*Ibid.*, pp. 128-130.
[9]Adoption of Customs Convention in London, 5 September 1944.
[10]"Yearbook of International Organizations," pp. 229-1125.

Ethics; International Relations; Social and Welfare; Professions and Employers; Commerce and Industry; Science; Health; Education and Youth.

Of the hundreds of international non-governmental organizations grouped in these eighteen categories, the author believes that the stature and aims of six combine to form a significant driving force toward eventual European political unity. Each is a symbol of unity in itself, and, when operating in unison, may make a major impact on the minds of millions of Europeans. Listed with the location of the headquarters of each, these institutions are:

1) Action Committee for a United States of Europe (ACUSE), Paris
2) Congress of the Peoples of Europe (CPE), Turin, Italy
3) European Cultural Centre (ECC), Geneva
4) European Movement (EM), Brussels
5) European Youth Campaign (EYC), Paris
6) Parliamentary Council of the European Movement (PCEM), Brussels

All six advocate steps toward some form of political unity. The activities of all six, along with scores of others, seem to be intensifying each year. Although the future course of action toward European unity is uncertain, and predictions hazardous, there are many signs and symbols which point in a common direction.

OUTSTANDING CONTEMPORARY SYMBOLS OF EUROPEAN UNITY.

Only by creating a united Europe would the peoples of the region be able to participate in world affairs in a manner commensurate with their history, their capacity for constructive leadership, and their aspirations for a better world order.

Committee on
*   International Policy*
National Planning Association
1962

1958-1962 EEC

European Economic Community, established 1958. The "Inner Six" or Common Market countries are: Belgium, France, Italy, Luxembourg, Netherlands, and West Germany.

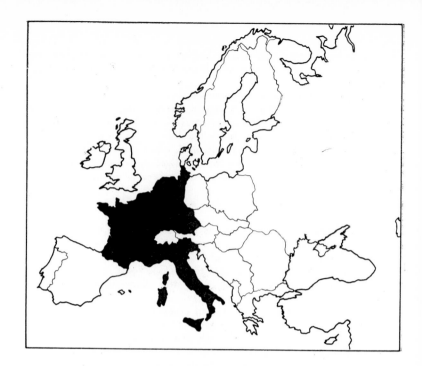

1960-1962 EFTA

European Free Trade Association, established 1960. The "Outer Seven" countries are: Austria, Denmark, Norway, Portugal, Sweden, Switzerland, and the United Kingdom.

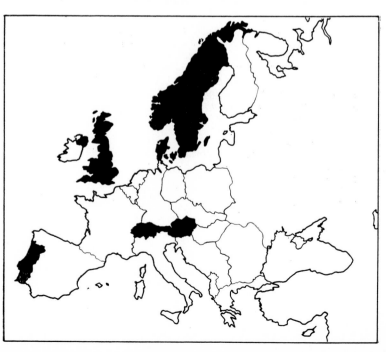

4

POTENTIAL AND ESSENTIALS FOR A

UNITED EUROPE

Throughout the centuries the level of human achievement attained by any people has usually been directly rooted in vision, imagination, initiative, hard work, perseverance, and faith. Of these six attributes, vision, human energy, and faith have reaped the most rewarding harvests. In addition to the creative utilization of human resources, the maturity of national vitality and of human achievement, culture, and enlightenment, have also depended upon the availability of the resources of nature. The great periods in history have been those where there has been deliberate, balanced, and constructive use of both human and natural resources in an attempt to achieve desirable and unselfish ends.

The potential human and natural resources for European unity are abundant and recognizable. The major resources might be listed as: natural, cultural, economic, social, political, and spiritual. Most of these resources have yet to be fully and widely understood, developed and appreciated. Within the major categories lie many secondary, but important resources: pride of nationalism (but willingness to cooperate internationally), pride of native language (still realizing the necessity for intergroup and international communication), pride of artistic and cultural heritage (yet willing to place ahead of stubborn pride the advantages of effective international cooperation, with individual and national sacrifices attendant thereto).

Each of the major resources listed above can be developed or otherwise utilized for the advantage of the greatest number of Europeans, if this development and utilization involves widespread cooperation and distribution of the advantages of development. To achieve the best and most abundant products from sound resource development, it is essential to have a harmonious merging of the natural resource elements. For full advantage, many of the natural resources now found in various European countries must be developed or processed at strategic centers, irrespective of present national boundaries. A review of the types, location, and variety of natural resources shows that sound economic exploitation of most of the resources is

EUROPE ABOUNDS IN RESOURCES ESSENTIAL FOR UNITY.

Freedom in a democracy is the glory of the State, and therefore in a democracy only will the freeman of nature deign to dwell.
Plato
427-347 B.C.

36

CULTURAL RESOURCES COMMON TO ALL OF EUROPE.

quite feasible if transport facilities can be made possible throughout Europe without economic restriction on raw materials, parts, or finished products.

The establishment (and wide support) of numerous international cultural organizations in Europe since the last war is striking evidence of the desire for, and the achievement of, cultural interchange between European countries. The cultural heritage of Europe has been unrestricted by artificial political boundaries for the last several centuries. The expansion and development of the cultural resources of all of Europe is both possible and desirable. The roots of many cultural resources are common in a number of European countries. Their continued international expansion and development would be natural if not restricted by artificial boundaries.

Likewise, the social resources and traditions of numerous European countries and sub-areas, have much in common. It would be desirable to preserve and encourage local and regional social customs and traditions. Local differences enrich and add color to society and in no way would conflict with international cooperation and unity.

EUROPE A RESERVOIR OF POLITICAL RESOURCES ESSENTIAL FOR UNITY.

Political resources abound. In fact, with the fragmentation of the continent into so many major and minor political subdivisions as now exist, one might conclude that there is an overabundance of political resources. Superfluous political institutions (all calling for staff) can throttle the economy of any society, and multiple governmental bureaucracy can lead to economic inflation and social decline. Countries have sometimes been choked by too much government and too much government intervention. Any move to simplify the political structure of Europe would in itself be a progressive step—with consequent economic and social benefits to the people of the entire continent.

EUROPE LACKING ESSENTIAL SPIRITUAL RESOURCES.

One of the neglected resources in Europe, as in America and elsewhere, is "spiritual." For the good of mankind in general, and for the peoples of Europe in particular, there must be a spiritual reawakening—a return to the basic belief in God, and to the teachings of Christ. In short, there must be a deep and widespread spiritual movement recalling the spirit which motivated the Reformation sparked by Martin Luther.

True Christianity, that ideology based directly on the teachings of Jesus Christ, is currently at a relatively low ebb in most countries in Europe. Unfortunately, this situation exists in much of the so-called Christian world. The tyrannical dogma propounded by the hierarchy of the Roman Catholic Church has little relation to true Christianity. Protestant State churches in England and Scandinavia, for the most part, have lost their zeal and spirituality. Lacking these virtues, the religions of much of Europe have had little moral impact on the lives of the vast majority of individuals.

The spread of communism and atheism among Europeans is a vivid demonstration of the moral ineffectiveness of both Roman Catholicism and the State churches.

If Europe would regain and retain her rightful place as a powerful and positive society among the peoples of the world, her only sure hope will be through a rebirth of the spirit of the Reformation. Strength, stability, and morality will only come to the European and to European society by way of a deep and widespread spiritual reformation—a true repudiation of the evils and errors of both atheism and Roman Catholicism.[1] A free and progressive Europe can only be achieved by the collaboration of free, God-fearing people.

REBIRTH OF RELIGIOUS FREEDOM ESSENTIAL FOR EUROPEAN UNITY.

Admitted or not, the fact remains that there is no other single force which has tended to shape the destinies of man through the centuries as has his religious philosophies (or the lack of them). The great migrations, the great buildings, the great artistic achievements, and, unfortunately, the great wars of history, have usually had their roots deep in the religious ideals and beliefs of people. And this is natural and logical. Man has ever sought a God; he was created with this built-in urge. If that place, designed for God in each individual, is not filled by His Spirit, it is usually filled with self. We need not understand the inner drives and desires of man to realize how man functions. The historical record of man and his works, both good and evil, are available to all who would seek to learn the truth.

Unity and freedom for the peoples of Europe can be achieved only through the continuous belief in, and adherence to, a spiritual and moral conduct which is now unfortunately lacking among all too many Europeans. A sweeping spiritual revival is not only one of the greatest needs of Europe, but it will be absolutely essential to any true and lasting form of unity, irrespective of the character of that unification.

EUROPE NEEDS SPIRITUAL REVIVAL TO ASSURE LASTING UNITY.

History has often shown that great men emerge to meet great challenges. It may be that men of the make-up of Reinold

---

[1]The following ideological forces are currently at work in Europe: Communism, Atheism, Roman Catholicism, Eastern Orthodoxy (Catholicism), Islamism, Judaism, Christianity. True Christians — those adhering to the teachings of Christ, are not tolerated by the Roman Catholic Hierarchy. Therefore, Roman Catholicism cannot (and should not) be classed as a truly Christian ideology. (See Appendix B.)

von Thadden-Trieglaff will lead Europe back to a God-fearing spiritual heritage. During the past decade von Thadden has sponsored a series of rallies throughout Central Europe known as "Kirchentags."[2] The impact of these rallies, and the numerous conferences and gatherings which grow out of these major meetings are resulting in a revitalization of the spiritual consciousness of hundreds of thousands. The practical consequences of this spiritual regeneration may well be one of the solid foundation stones upon which a united Europe can be built.

Throughout history, nations and peoples of strength and vitality have had deep moral and spiritual convictions. Coupled with high national purposes, rooted in political and religious freedom, deep moral and spiritual convictions will be both steppingstones and keystones to European unity.

[2]Clarence W. Hall, "He Gave a Nation Back Its Soul," Reader's Digest, January 1962, pp. 113-117.

We cannot possibly exist if we reject the time-honored moral absolutes of the Ten Commandments and the Sermon on the Mount. The Scripture says, "Righteousness exalteth a nation, but sin is a reproach to any people."
Billy Graham
1960

5

CONTEMPORARY VIEWS ON EUROPEAN

UNITY

In the bibliography of the recently published "N.A.T.O. and the European Union Movement" by Professor M. Margaret Ball,[1] 529 references are listed. Although many of these sources relate to NATO, it appears that an equal number relate more specifically to the European Union Movement. Since Professor Ball completed the manuscript for her book in December of 1958, at least several scores of additional documents have been published on some phase of this intensifying problem. Thus, the mere fact of the emergence of this extensive library (mostly during the past 15 years) is conclusive evidence of the significance of European unity.

Without attempting to appraise the content of many of the publications on the subject, or to refer necessarily to the more voluminous of the popular works, it might be advantageous to mention a few of the more important ones.

Reference sources might be grouped in four major categories: a) Addresses; b) Articles and editorials in newspapers and periodicals; c) Reports of committees or agencies; and d) Books.

Prominent among the addresses in which some form of European unity was advocated, were several given by Sir Winston Churchill. One of his earlier and most notable speeches was delivered at Westminster College in Fulton, Missouri, on 5 March 1946. In the stirring address on that occasion he said: "The safety of the world requires a new unity in Europe, from which no nation should be permanently outcast. It is from the quarrels of the strong parent races in Europe that the world wars we have witnessed, or which occurred in former times, have sprung. . . . Surely we should work with conscious purpose for a grand pacification of Europe, within the structure of the United Nations and in accordance with its Charter. That I feel is open cause of policy of very great importance."[2]

EUROPEAN UNITY IS "IN THE AIR" AND THE SUBJECT OF COUNTLESS BOOKS.

MAJOR REFERENCE SOURCES ON EUROPEAN UNITY.

CHURCHILL ADVOCATES UNITY.

---

[1]M. Margaret Ball, "N.A.T.O. and the European Union Movement" (New York: Frederick A. Praeger, Inc., 1959), 486 pp.
[2]Randolph S. Churchill, Editor, "The Sinews of Peace: Post-War Speeches by Sir Winston S. Churchill" (London: Cassell & Co., Ltd., 1948), pp. 101-102.

CHURCHILL'S FAMOUS ADDRESS IN ZURICH.

One of the most widely heralded of Churchill's addresses was that given at the University of Zurich on 19 September 1946. From many viewpoints, it was a startling speech—recommending action which at first sounded fantastic, but which was soon judged to be logical. In part, he said: "If Europe were once united in the sharing of its common inheritance, there would be no limit to the happiness, to the prosperity and the glory which its three or four hundred million people would enjoy."[3]

In yet another address, given on 21 April 1948, in the Royal Albert Hall in London, Churchill warned: "There can be no hope for the world unless the peoples of Europe unite together to preserve their freedom, their culture and their civilization, founded upon Christian ethics."[4]

In somewhat the same vein, in a speech in The Hague on 7 May 1948, Churchill stated: "Europe can only be united by the heartfelt wish and vehement expression of the great majority of all the peoples in all the parties in all the freedom-loving countries, no matter where they dwell or how they vote."[5]

CHURCHILL BACKS COUNT COUDENHOVE-KALERGI'S PROPOSAL FOR UNITY.

On numerous occasions, Churchill pleaded for unity for the peoples and nations of Europe. His staunch and continued backing of this idea was perhaps one of the primary forces which stimulated others to help carry the torch of European unity. He also took every opportunity to encourage others in their attempts to develop greater interest in this vital subject. He gladly accepted the invitation of Count Coudenhove-Kalergi to write an introduction to the Count's book entitled, "An Idea Conquers the World."[6] Churchill concludes this introduction with the following paragraph, "The movement towards European solidarity which has now begun will not stop until it has effected tremendous and possibly decisive changes in the whole life, thought, and structure of Europe. It does not follow even that this progress will be gradual. It may leap forward in a huge bound on spontaneous conviction. It may even prove to be the surest means of lifting the mind of European nations out of the ruck of old feuds and ghastly revenges. It may afford a rallying ground where socialists and capitalists, where nationalists and pacifists, where idealists and business men may stand together. It may be the surest of all guarantees against the renewal of great wars."

---

[3]Andrew and Frances Body, "Western Union" (Washington, D.C.,: Public Affairs Press, 1949), pp. 109-112.
[4]F. B. Czarnomski, Editor, "The Wisdom of Winston Churchill" (London: Allen & Unwin, 1956), p. 129.
[5]*Ibid.*, p. 129.
[6]Count Coudenhove-Kalergi, "An Idea Conquers the World" (London: Hutchinson & Co., 1953), pp. ix-x.

Another leading figure in the Western World to stress the advisability of a United Europe was President Eisenhower. Perhaps his most forthright statement on the subject was contained in an address given at the commencement exercises at Baylor University in Waco, Texas, on 25 May 1956, when he declared:

"The statesmen of Western Europe have long been aware that only in broad and effective cooperation among the nations of that region can true security for all be found. They know that real unification of the separate countries there would make their combined 250 million highly civilized people a mighty pillar of free strength in the modern world. A free United States of Europe would be strong in the skills of its people, adequately endowed with natural resources, and rich in their common culture and artistic heritage. It would be a highly prosperous community.

"Without such unification the history of the past half century in Europe could go on in dreary repetition, possibly to the ultimate destruction of all the values those people themselves hold most dear. With unification, a new sun of hope, security and confidence would shine for Europe, for us, and for the free world.

"Another stumbling block to European unity is the failure of populations as a whole to grasp the long-term political, economic and security advantage of union. These are matters that do not make for a soul-stirring address on a national holiday. They can be approached only in thought, in wisdom—almost, I think we may say, in prayer.

"Nevertheless—and happily—much progress has been made.

"Years ago, our European partners began both to study and to act. Our country's help was given wherever possible because our own future security and prosperity are inescapably linked to those of our European friends. There was established the Brussels Compact, the Organization for European Economic Cooperation, the European Payments Union, the European Coal and Steel Community, and the Council for Europe. The North Atlantic Treaty Organization—NATO—although an organization comprehending much more than Western Europe, nonetheless provides the cooperative mechanism for greater security in the area. All these were set up to attack immediate problems in cooperation.

"Despite setbacks and difficulties, these have been operating with increasing efficiency. So, European Union, one of the greatest dreams of Western man, seems nearer today than at any time in centuries, providing bright promise for

EISENHOWER RECOMMENDS UNIFICATION OF EUROPE.

The leader of a democracy is not the source of power; he merely directs it. Power derives from, and must remain in, the people.
Dwight D. Eisenhower
1962

the future of our European friends and for the growth and strength of liberty."[7]

British statesmen and business leaders continue to urge European unity. Three rather recent speeches are striking evidence of this fact.

GEBB SEES UNITY ESSENTIAL FOR EUROPEAN SURVIVAL.

Upon his retirement from the British Foreign Service, and from his post as Ambassador to France, Sir Gladwyn Gebb addressed the Anglo-American Press Club in Paris on 7 September 1960. In the course of his remarks (on the subject of two European economic blocs), Lord Gladwyn states:

". . . The various states of Western Europe, of which, if only from the point of view of geography, the United Kingdom is naturally a part, cannot for political and historical reasons, be divided without weakening the whole structure of Western Society. . . . There is the final consideration that for so long as Western Europe is divided into two potential 'blocs' the Soviet Union in the long run will have little difficulty in playing off one against the other. All of the countries of Western Europe without exception have their special weaknesses and it is only if they bind themselves together that they can hope to avoid the temptation of indulging them. . . .

"It is indeed commonly said, and with reason, that the economic difficulties in the way of a fresh start to negotiations for a United Europe, though formidable, are soluble, given good will.

". . . Now, therefore, seems to be the time when schemes should be canvassed and active public consideration given to all projects for arriving at greater European cooperation. . . . But what frightens me is that unless a real effort is soon made to achieve the politico-economic unity of Western Europe we shall 'all' (and I mean without exception) go into a slow decline in comparison with the 'bloc' of the Eastern Countries. And we know in our hearts where such a process must inevitably lead. It will lead to the disruption of the Occident and to the triumph of Communism."[8]

HEATH SUGGESTS ECONOMIC UNITY IS PRIMARILY POLITICAL.

At the meeting in Strasbourg of the Consultative Assembly of the Council of Europe on 27 September 1960, the British Lord Privy Seal, the Rt. Hon. Edward Heath, M.B.E., M.P., was speaking on the need for developing closer ties between the countries of the free world. He had just made the point that Europe and America are bound together for mutual security reasons. He

---

[7]From a Press Release from the White House, in Washington, D.C., dated 25 May 1956.

[8]From a mimeographed copy of the speech by Lord Gladwyn (Sir Gladwyn Gebb) provided by the British Embassy in Paris.

43

went on to say,

"Furthermore, we Europeans must ourselves move ever more closely together. Amid the present strains and tensions it is unwarrantable luxury for us to indulge in dissensions.

"That is why I say that the reasons for our concern about the economic division of Europe are primarily political. When we consider dispassionately the situation of the European peoples in the world today we cannot fail to be struck by the contrast between the success of their economic recovery and the increasing difficulties of their political situation.

". . . It seems to me that however varied may be the groupings and associations which we make within the European family, there remains a residue of joint responsibility and of common action which we ought constantly to keep in mind. I feel that all our associations, whether it be the Council of Europe, or W.E.U., or the European Economic Community, or the European Free Trade Association, ought all to be regarded as contributory to the basic unity of Europe, and that we ought to make sure that we do not allow them to create fundamental divisions between us.

"The British Government seriously believes that the existence of the two groupings—the E.E.C. and the EFTA—is in danger of creating a serious division of this kind. . . .

"What we fear is that the economic split will lead inevitably to political disruption, to rival political allegiances and to growing suspicion and estrangement of two parts of Europe.

". . . As Mr. Selwyn Lloyd said at this Assembly in January: 'We, in Britain regard ourselves as part of Europe. By history, by tradition, by civilization, by sentiment, by geography, we are part of Europe.'

". . . The creation of the Six (EEC) has revealed a new dynamic in European history. In its enthusiasm and sense of purpose it is answering a yearning for something greater than the individual nation state which has long existed in European hearts and minds. . . . We want to play our part in the developing unity of this Continent."[19]

In complete harmony with other British leaders of the recent past and of the present, Prime Minister Harold Macmillan has on many occasions stated his belief in, and hope for, the unity of Europe. His speech before the Assembly of the

. . . In democracies of the more extreme type, there has arisen a false idea of freedom which is contradictory to the true interests of the state . . . Men think that what is just is equal; and that equality is the supremacy of the popular will; and that freedom is the doing of what man likes . . . But this is all wrong; men should not think it slavery to live according to the rule of the constitution; for it is their salvation.

Aristotle
384-322 B.C.

MACMILLAN A STAUNCH ADVOCATE OF EUROPEAN UNITY.

[9]From a mimeographed copy of the speech by the Lord Privy Seal, the Rt. Hon. Edward Heath, M.B.E., M.P., to the Consultative Assembly of the Council of Europe, Strasbourg, 27 September 1960. Copy supplied by the New York Office of the British Information Service.

Western European Union, meeting at Church House, Westminster, London, on the 29th of May, 1961, set forth his philosophy and convictions on the subject. On that occasion he said, in part:

"European history, as perhaps all history, seems to move in cycles. At the end of the Middle Ages the rise of extreme nationalism coincided more or less with the recognition of Europe's supremacy and the defeat of her only dangerous enemies. It is therefore not surprising that the new challenge to Europe and the new threats to our ideals and our way of life should have forced us again to think more of our unity than of our diversity.

"In the present movement towards unity in Europe there is another feature which is truly unique. There have been past federations or empires or groupings within Europe, but they have always been the result of war, of force, of conquest, or of dynastic alliance. I do not know of another case in which they have been built spontaneously. The Empire of Charlemagne, the Empire of the Hapsburgs, the Confederation of the Rhine were all imposed from above. This time the growth of unity has been natural, I repeat spontaneous and not imposed. It is scarcely surprising that the growth of the tree of unity with its deep roots in all our countries should have been slower than that of the ephemeral structures of the past.

"There are great difficulties in creating new sytems, as you all know, among proud and independent nations with developed and highly evolved cultures. I am not surprised at this, but I am not disheartened. I believe that our goal is clear ahead, and that it is within our grasp. It is to create the maximum unity in Europe and beyond. This unity must be sought in all fields of human activity. In reaching it we must accept the special position of different countries, each of which has a different contribution to make. If unity is our aim, and if we keep it firmly before us, I do not doubt that we shall succeed—and succeed perhaps sooner than some pessimists may believe. Meanwhile, let us not harp on the difficulties and divisions but think rather of the fundamental purposes and traditions which inspire us all.

". . . We firmly believe that Europe should be united. We must ever have in our hearts the hope that some day, by peaceful evolution, this will mean not half Europe but all Europe—East and West. For we must never forget the cruel division that separates the Eastern and Western countries of Europe.

"Meanwhile, we are determined to press forward with the consolidation of Western Europe . . .

"Perhaps you will allow me one last reflection. Sitting in this City and this building, where for a period of the war we held our British Parliament after the destruction of our own, let us not think too pessimistically of the difficulties of today. Let us count our blessings. No one who went around Europe in the summer of 1945, as I did, would have dreamed that in sixteen short years there could have been such a transformation. We have rebuilt our own countries. We need not fear that the European genius no longer flowers. In spite of all the dangers and troubles ahead, we no longer doubt the contribution which the old world can and will make to the peaceful development of all nations. I am sure that this Assembly, in its meetings here in London, will contribute worthily to the next stage. I count it a great honor that you have allowed me to speak, and I venture to give you and all my colleagues, respectfully but sincerely, my best wishes and hopes for leading us along the path to unity."[10]

On 13 November 1961, Prime Minister Macmillan once again expressed his faith and hope in unity. He also expressed the belief that this unity would result in good, rather than harm, to the British Commonwealth. In the course of his remarks at the Lord Mayor's annual banquet in the Guildhall in London on the 13th, he said:

"The Government believes that we can strengthen our links with Europe—in every field—without injury to, and indeed with great ultimate benefit for, the whole Commonwealth. To that end—we are presently engaged in negotiations of historic significance. We do not yet know whether they will succeed. I trust they will; I believe they must. For if Europe does not achieve this degree of unity and common purpose, there is little chance of our rising to the challenge of today."[11]

Britain's decision to attempt to enter the European Common Market was disturbing to the other Commonwealth countries, at least until recently. On 10 September 1962, the first of a series of closed-door conferences started in London which was attended by the leaders of the Commonwealth countries

Call it religion, patriotism, sympathy, the enthusiasm for humanity or the love of God — give it what name you will; there is yet a force which is the electricity of the moral universe; a force besides which all others are weak. . . . And this force of forces — that now goes to waste or assumes perverted forms — we may use for the strengthening and building up and ennobling of society, if we but will, just as we now use physical forces that once seemed but powers of destruction. All we have to do is but give it freedom and scope.

Henry George
1839-1897

[10]From a mimeographed copy of the speech by the Prime Minister, the Rt. Hon. Harold Macmillan, M.P., at the opening of the Assembly of Western European Union on Monday, 29th May 1961 at Church House, Westminster. Copy of speech supplied by the New York Office of the British Information Service.

[11]From a mimeographed copy of the speech by the Prime Minister, the Rt. Hon. Harold Macmillan, M.P., at the Lord Mayor's Banquet, Guildhall, on Monday, 13 November 1961. Copy supplied by the New York Office of the British Information Services.

With malice toward none, with charity for all, with firmness in the right as God gives to us to see the right, let us strive on to finish the work we are in, to bind up the nation's wounds, to care for him who shall have borne the battle and for his widow and his orphan, to do all which may achieve and cherish a just and lasting peace among ourselves and with all nations.

*Abraham Lincoln
1865*

and representatives of Britain. After a week of serious sessions, the Commonwealth countries were finally convinced that the British Isles, by the nature of their location, would have to remain an integral part of Europe, and that the very political and economic life of Britain was directly related to—and dependent upon—the political and economic life of the whole of Europe. The Commonwealth leaders came to the logical conclusion that the future relationship of Britain to the rest of Western Europe will have to be determined by Britain and her European neighbors, and not by the Commonwealth countries.

While none of the talks during the Commonwealth conference were made public, Prime Minister Macmillan addressed the nation on the 20th of September with a summary of the talks and his opinions on their significance. In part, the Prime Minister said:[12a]

". . . There is no direct political commitment in the Common Market, but, of course, it is one of the objects of the member countries to grow closer together politically, and naturally as their economic growth comes together, so will their political.

"But what we have been discussing with the Commonwealth is really this: it's how to reconcile the strong historical structure of the Commonwealth and the new developing structure on the continent of Europe.

"This isn't really essentially a new problem for us, because all through our history, combined with all the immense outward growth of the British people, all over the world, we've still been very much involved in Europe's affairs. We can't escape it. Sometimes we've tried to—but we can't.

"Now it's no good pretending. Some people naturally feel like this. That we can go back to the old world, before the war. A lot of people do look backward, but the real test you must bring to this question is are we going to look forward?

"A year ago the British Government decided—and it was a great decision—to start to talk and negotiate with the European Community, to see whether we could deal with the situation by joining the Common Market ourselves, on terms which would be both honourable and acceptable. And we took this great decision for two reasons. One political, the other economic.

"Politically, because we were very glad to see the end of Europe's quarrels. Quarrels in which we've been tragically

---

[12a]From a mimeographed copy of the transcribed TV recordings. Copy furnished by the Office of the Prime Minister in Admiralty House, London.

involved throughout history. Twice in my lifetime. Because we wanted to strengthen the new unity in Europe. And also because we knew that if we were not in Europe our influence would begin to decline, and with the decline of our influence in Europe we should lose our influence in the world outside.

". . . A political reason, a great historic reason, why we made this decision. To preserve the power and strength of Britain in the world.

". . . British industry will have to concentrate more and more on the complicated, sophisticated, specialised goods. Not just the things which almost anybody can learn to make, but the difficult things which need great precision, and highly skilled workmen.

"And yet it's just these very industries, which also require immense investment of capital. Very high investment of capital is required for very highly developed and very specialised plants . . . Now the Europeans are going to have a home market of nearly 200 million people. Even now, perhaps more. How are we going to sell this kind of produce? Either to the Europeans in the Common Market area, or outside to the other markets in the world, in competition with the Europeans. How are we going to sell them if the base, the home market, is only a quarter of theirs?

"When we know the final position then it will be for us here in Britain to decide what to do. All the Commonwealth have accepted that fact. Because, after all, we're independent, too, if it comes to that.

"So, we want to preserve, and strengthen the Commonwealth. We want also to play our part in Europe. Many of us, especially those who are young in heart, or in years, are impatient of the old disputes; intolerant of the obsolete conceptions; anxious that our country should take its part, and if possible a leading part, in all these new and hopeful movements. All over Western Europe people are looking to Britain to join them in this work of peace and progress. And given the right terms of entry I am sure this is the right way ahead for us."

On 9 October 1962, a 10-page booklet entitled "Britain the Commonwealth and Europe" was published by the Conservative and Unionist Central Office in London.[12b] The booklet, prepared by Prime Minister Macmillian, summarizes his opinions on the relationship of Britain to Europe, and clearly states the case

. . . we may define a republic to be, or at least may bestow that name on, a government which derives all its powers directly or indirectly from the great body of the people, and is administered by persons holding their offices during pleasure, for a limited period, or during good behaviour. It is ESSENTIAL *to such a government that it be derived from the great body of the society, not from an inconsiderable proportion, or a favoured class of it. . . .*
James Madison
1787

[12b]The Right Hon. Harold Macmillan, M.P., "Britain the Commonwealth and Europe" (London: Conservative and Unionist Office, N.D. 10 pages. Issued on 9 October 1962).

for both his party and the majority of the people of Britain. In part the Prime Minister writes:

"By joining this vigorous and expanding community (European Community) and becoming one of its leading members, as I am convinced we would, this country would not only gain a new stature in Europe, but also increase its standing and influence in the councils of the world. We would bring to the inward preoccupations of a continental land mass the outward-looking vision of a great trading nation whose political and economic horizons span the globe."

The concluding paragraph of this booklet reads:

"To many of us, and to our younger generation in particular, the time is past for harping on old disputes and nursing obsolete conceptions. We want to see Britain taking the lead in building a new future and working towards that unity of the world which is the ultimate vision of mankind. The European Community is a signpost to that future and we must play our part."

PAUL HENRI SPAAK AND UNITY.

Paul Henri Spaak of Belgium has long been an advocate of a united Europe. In contrast to many European leaders, M. Spaak favors the creation of a European nation with strong central powers. He is also opposed to any national governmental organization which would call for unanimous agreement on major issues. In a speech delivered in New York City on 25 January 1962, M. Spaak stated, "The more I see, the more I travel and the greater my political experience, the more I grow hostile to international organizations in which the rule of unanimity reigns. . . . I cannot conceive of a normally and efficiently functioning Europe unless all powers accept the rule of the majority."

KENNEDY PROPOSES EUROPEAN UNITY AND TIES WITH AMERICA.

Still another world leader to take note of the forces of unity in Europe is President John F. Kennedy of the USA. In an historic address delivered in front of Independence Hall in Philadelphia on the 4th of July, 1962, he stated in part:

"The nations of Western Europe, long divided by feuds more bitter than any which existed among the thirteen colonies, are joining together, seeking as our forefathers sought, to find freedom in diversity and unity in strength. The United States looks on this vast new enterprise with hope and admiration. We do not regard a strong and united Europe as a rival but as a partner. To aid its progress has been the basic objective of our foreign policy for seventeen years. We believe that a united Europe will be capable of playing a greater role in the common defense, of responding more generously to the needs of poorer nations, of joining with the United

States and others in lowering trade barriers, resolving problems of currency and commodities, and developing coordinated policies in all other economic, diplomatic and political areas. We see in such a Europe a partner with whom we could deal on a basis of full equality in all great and burdensome tasks of building and defending a community of free nations. . . . The first order of business is for our European friends to go forward in forming a more perfect union which will some day make this partnership possible."[13]

Articles and editorials in newspapers and periodicals on some phase of European unity are far too numerous to list or refer to in detail. Journals and newspapers in both Europe and America have been presenting news reports, editorials, analyses, reviews, and proposals and possibilities in almost a continuous stream over the past number of years on some phase of cooperation among the countries of Europe. While much of this writing has related to economic cooperation, the economic blocs, the industrial recovery of Western Europe, and the increasing reduction of trade barriers between the nations of Europe, there have also been many serious articles on the basic problems and possibilities of European political unity. While the reference sources available to the author have been primarily in English language publications, there is good reason to believe that there has been an equally wide coverage in magazines and papers printed in other languages.

EUROPEAN UNITY A FAVORITE PRESS SUBJECT.

During the past two years The New York Times has given considerable editorial space to the topic of European unity. Without attempting to summarize or quote from these editorials, the mere reproduction of the titles under which they were written gives an excellent clue to the content. The principal editorials in The Times (New York) appeared as follows: 3 June 1960 "Europe's Search for Unity;" 2 August 1960 "Europe's Road to Unity;" 13 August 1960 "Britain joins Europe;" 15 October 1960 "Europe's Search for Unity;" 1 March 1961 "Britain's Bid to Europe;" 2 August 1961 "Britain Crosses the Channel."

An excellent feature-length article by Robert C. Doty appeared on page E-5 of the New York Times on 7 August 1960 under the title "Europe Seeks Unity: World Tensions Spur the Search for Closer Ties That Would Increase Continent's Strength."

The editorial page of the New York Times of 8 July 1962 included a lengthy editorial on the recent discussions between

EDITORS OF NEW YORK TIMES DEVOTE MUCH SPACE TO EUROPEAN UNITY.

---

[13]From a mimeographed copy of the address by President Kennedy as it was actually delivered on 4 July 1962 in front of Independence Hall, Philadelphia, Pennsylvania. (Copy supplied by The White House Press Secretary.)

President de Gaulle and Chancellor Adenauer on the potential roles of their two countries in a united Europe and the relationship of Britain both to the Common Market and to France and Germany as these major powers negotiate for their respective places in what appears to be a European political union.

HEALTHY ECONOMIC ENVIRONMENT ESSENTIAL TO UNITY SAYS U. S. NEWS & WORLD REPORT.

The roots of stability and unity lie in large part in a healthy economic environment. An article in "U.S. News & World Report" of July 10 1961 (pages 54-57), under the title "Europe's Amazing Boom - Can U.S. Match It?" indicates clearly that these economic foundations are sound and that the generally attractive economic picture throughout Western Europe is equally firmly based. As one reviews the fact that the United States of America grew in strength and unity during the last half of the 19th century when it was experiencing a period of economic growth, one might contemplate whether the forces of unity in America a century ago were similar to the forces at work in Europe today. Granted that European nationalism and conservatism might be stumbling blocks which were not in evidence in America, there is still the possibility that the economic forces now at play might out-balance some of the non-unifying forces.

TIME MAGAZINE FEATURES JEAN MONNET AND HIS ROLE IN EUROPEAN UNITY.

An even more pointed article appeared in "Time" magazine on 6 October 1961. The headline on the cover of this issue of Time read, "New Strength for the West: Europe Unites in the Common Market." The article following, which appeared on pages 28 - 33, is in part a story of Jean Monnet, perhaps the chief apostle of European unity. It was Monnet who planned the Coal and Steel Community. It was Monnet who conceived the Common Market. Monnet continues to be one of Europe's leading teachers and preachers of unity. The article also describes, by word and illustration, several of the European international organizations, their roles and success.

By far the largest volume of printed material on the various problems related to cooperation between the nations of Europe is in the form of reports of the activities of numerous organizations, committees, and conferences which have dealt with some phase of the question of unity. Many of these bodies have regular meetings, and from each gathering has come a record of its proceedings. The work of most committees has taken the form of committee reports. Obviously, much of this material is a record of the debates which have ensued. Many diverse views have been recorded. Committees have been hard at work gathering figures, recording opinions, and drafting proposals. Scores of reports are actually records of the progress of the several international organizations.

It would be of little value here to try any analysis of this mass of material. However, it might be noted that after the smoke has cleared from the fiery debates, and after the committee reports have been presented, argued and recorded, there has emerged during the past few years a series of recommendations, actions, agreements, documents, and organizations, all of which, when reviewed from an objective standpoint, form a cohesive foundation essential for, and indicative of, ever greater unity between the countries of Europe. There can be no disputing the fact that substantial progress toward unity has been made.

But even more important, this progress has emerged from the open debates on the scores of related questions, from the spontaneous exchange of views, from an atmosphere wherein the participants for the first time in European history have earnestly attempted to cooperate toward the common goal of unity without the force of arms. The uniqueness of this cooperative environment gives rise to the hope that at long last the countries of Europe might seriously seek to pool their resources to subdue their nationalism for the achievement of a greater cause—a peaceful and unified Europe.

That literally scores of books have been published during the past 25 years, dealing with some phase of the question of cooperation between European countries, is evidence that the idea has been deemed worthy of serious consideration.

Many volumes have been the direct outgrowth of the activities and programs of international organizations. Still others are devoted to describing and appraising the work of one or more of these bodies. Another group of books has undertaken an evaluation of the European Union Movement. Yet another category, and one containing some of the more interesting reading, is where authors have undertaken to propose avenues which they believe might lead to some form of unity.

At the risk of omitting other worthy sources, there are five volumes which are outstanding in the category of those describing and appraising the work of one or more of the organizations in the European Union Movement:

1) "European Institutions" by A. H. Robertson,[14] presents an excellent description of the structure and functions of fifteen of the more important European organizations with some information about their principal activities. The extensive appendix includes the institutional provisions of the treaties by which the

Justice and freedom; discussion and criticism; intelligence and character — these are the indispensable ingredients of the democratic state.

Robert M. Hutchins
1960

LIBRARY OF BOOKS WRITTEN ON EUROPEAN COOPERATION AND UNITY.

"EUROPEAN INSTITUTIONS" BY ROBERTSON.

---

[14]A. H. Robertson, "European Institutions" (London: Stevens & Sons, 1959), 372 pp. (Published under the auspices of The London Institute of World Affairs.)

fifteen organizations noted have been created. The usefulness of the volume is enhanced by the opening chapter entitled "The Development of European Integration," and by the closing chapter "The Rationalization of European Institutions."

"THE COUNCIL OF EUROPE" BY ROBERTSON.

2) "The Council of Europe," also by A. H. Robertson,[15] is a comprehensive exposition on the structure, functions, and achievements of one of the most dominant forces working toward the unity of Europe—The Council of Europe.

"N.A.T.O. AND THE EUROPEAN UNION MOVEMENT" BY BALL.

3) "N.A.T.O. and the European Union Movement," by M. Margaret Ball,[16] is an extensive treatment of the forces and institutions related to the integration of Europe and of Europe to the broader Atlantic community under NATO. One feature of the volume of special value is the extensive bibliography listing over 500 references.

"EUROPEAN ASSEMBLIES" BY LINDSAY.

4) "European Assemblies," by Kenneth Lindsay,[17] presents a critical analysis of the development of the international parliamentary assemblies movement over the experimental years from 1949 to 1959. The author outlines the significance and functioning of these novel bodies and indicates many of the difficulties inherent in the overlapping activities of these rather peculiar international organizations.

"THE STRUGGLE TO UNITE EUROPE" BY ZURCHER.

5) "The Struggle to Unite Europe, 1940 - 1958," by Arnold J. Zurcher,[18] is an excellent summary of the movement to unite Europe, from its origins in the Pan-European Union to the drafting of the treaties for Euratom and the European Common Market. It is a record of the emergence of the movement from the realm of wishful thinking to the reality of practical politics.

OTHER SIGNIFICANT BOOKS ON EUROPEAN UNITY.

One other group of books provides stimulating reading. In nearly every case, the opening sections of the book present a review of the European movement toward unity, but the author then goes on to advocate some form of action or organization which he believes might be a logical avenue leading to greater unity. The titles of these volumes indicate the principal theme of the book, and this is sufficient for the purpose of the present study. In two instances individuals of world renown have seen fit to write introductions. The books are listed here in chronological order: "Pan-Europe," by Richard N. Coudenhove-Kalergi,

[15]A. H. Robertson, "The Council of Europe" (New York: Frederick A. Praeger, Second Edition, 1961), 298 pp. (Published under the auspices of the London Institute of World Affairs.)
[16]M. Margaret Ball, "N.A.T.O. and the European Movement" (New York: Frederick A. Praeger, 1959), 486 pp.
[17]Kenneth Lindsay, "European Assemblies" (London: Stevens & Sons, Ltd., 1960), 267 pp.
[18]Arnold J. Zurcher, "The Struggle to Unite Europe, 1940-1958" (New York: New York University Press, 1958), 254 pp.

with an introduction by Nicholas Murray Butler, 1926; "Union Now - A Proposal for Atlantic Federal Union of the Free," by Clarence K. Streit, first edition, 1940, second edition, 1949; "The State of Europe," by Howard K. Smith, 1949; "An Idea Conquers the World," by Count Coudenhove-Kalergi, with an introduction by Sir Winston Churchill, 1953; "How Can Europe Survive?" by Hans F. Sennholz, 1955; "Europe Will Not Wait - A Warning and a Way Out," by Anthony Nutting, 1960.

The overriding theme in this growing library is European unity. Objections have been raised in many quarters, and obstacles have been placed along the road to unity; but as more and more leaders of the countries of Western Europe are convinced of the wisdom of international cooperation, the tide is beginning to turn on all fronts to the acceptance of the idea. The demonstration of the value of economic unity may well pave the way for political unity. If international cooperation between the European countries moves as fast during the next five years as it has during the past five years, there is no telling what may happen.

Whether we realize it or not, we may now be witnessing the beginning of a new nation—the United Countries of Europe.

How does one contribute to the greatness and strength of a free society? That is a question to which there are many true answers. One answer is — pursue excellence! Those who are most devoted to a democratic society must be precisely the ones who insist that free men are capable of the highest standards of performance, that a free society can be a great society in the richest sense of that phrase. The idea for which this nation stands will not survive if the highest goal free man can set themselves is an amiable mediocrity.

John W. Gardner
1960

6

REFLECTIONS ON A GOVERNMENTAL STRUCTURE FOR A NEW NATION

God governs the world, and we have only to do our duty wisely, and leave the issue to him.
John Jay
1745-1829

STRONG CENTRAL GOVERNMENT VS. CONFEDERATION.

Government is a trust, and the officers of government are trustees; and both the trust and the trustees are created for the benefit of the people.
Henry Clay
1829

DRAFT CONSTITUTION PROPOSED FOR A "UNITED STATES OF EUROPE."

Already several proposals have been advocated for a specific form of government of a new nation uniting the countries of Western Europe: these have ranged from proposals for a rather loosely knit "federation" to a "United States of Europe," with strong central governmental administration. Some have felt that the pattern of uniting followed in the United States of America, could apply to the countries of Europe. However, others have been quick to point out that many of the factors which were common to the American colonies do not exist in Europe—one of the chief being the lack of a common language.

There have been scores of conflicting views on the pros and cons of every phase of international cooperation between the European countries. If one were to tabulate the advantages and possibilities against the disadvantages and impossibilities—in light of the progress which has been made—the scoring would heavily favor the potential for cooperation. There has been a good deal of debate on what form of international cooperation might be achieved. Even a firm nationalist, like President Charles de Gaulle, has claimed that political unity would be easier to achieve than economic unity.

Since this statement, French leaders, both in and out of government, have completely changed their attitude, and are now completely convinced of the advantages of economic unity. France is currently one of the leading supporters of the European Common Market, and is even now coming to the point of realizing that there should be only ONE economic organization embracing all of the countries of Western Europe—including Britain. If a strong nationalist country such as France can shift its reasoning, it is not impossible that political unity, as well as economic unity, can be achieved.

Perhaps the most specific form of government to be proposed for Western Europe is expressed in a "Draft Constitution of the United States of Europe" and published as an appendix in the book by Arnold J. Zurcher, "The Struggle to Unite Europe,

1940-1958."[13] This draft constitution is primarily the work of four men: Messrs. Fernando de los Rios and Stephen P. Ladas, representing the Judicial Committee of the Pan-European Conference, and Messrs. Richard Coudenhove-Kalergi and Arnold J. Zurcher, representing the Research Seminar for European Federation; New York University. Prepared in New York City and dated 25 March 1944, this draft constitution comprises a preamble and 95 articles grouped under fifteen sections. A brief idea of the content of this proposed constitution may be drawn from the titles of the several sections: 1) The United States and the Union; 2) Internal Constitutional Standards of Member States; 3) Interstate Relations; 4) The Rights of the Individual; 5) Social Rights; 6) Defense; 7) Foreign Affairs; 8) Colonial Territories; 9) Economic Policy; 10) Revenues of the Union; 11) The Congress; 12) The Council; 13) The Supreme Court; 14) Accession to the Union-Transitional Provision; 15) Amendment and Revision.

There is considerable virtue in the draft constitution as set forth by the four gentlemen. However, since 1944, conditions and attitudes have changed considerably in Europe, and the same authors would doubtless make numerous changes in any similar document which they might prepare today—even though the fundamentals may remain primarily the same.

It is not the objective of the present volume to propose any specific form of governmental structure, but rather to advance the idea that some form of political coalition may well emerge, and, irrespective of the type of union, a central grouping of the numerous governmental bodies, departments, councils, courts, and the many other related organizations, agencies, and staffs, would add efficiency and effectiveness to any and all cooperative efforts in government.

To avoid possible lack of distinction, it is recommended that neither the term "nation" nor "state" be used in the name of the new country. "Nation" would tend to confuse the new union with the United Nations Organization (UNO or UN); while "state" would be easily mistaken for the United States of America (USA or US). It is recommended that the name of the new union be the "United Countries of Europe" (UCE). This name would be unique, avoid confusion, signify unity, and, at the same time, emphasize the fact that the new nation is a grouping of 'countries' with all the implied meaning of so-called "States' rights."

---

[1]Arnold J. Zurcher, "The Struggle to Unite Europe, 1940-1958" (New York: New York University Press, 1958), 254 pages.

We hold these truths to be self-evident, that all men are created equal, but that they are endowed by their Creator with certain unalienable Rights, that among these are Life, Liberty and the pursuit of Happiness. — That to secure these rights, Governments are instituted among Men, deriving their just powers from the consent of the governed.

Declaration of Independence 1776
(Drafted by Thomas Jefferson)

Government . . . is that POWER by which individuals in society are kept from doing injury to each other, and are brought to co-operate to a common end.
Alexander Hamilton 1794

UNITED COUNTRIES OF EUROPE PROPOSED AS NAME FOR NEW NATION.

AVOID STRONG CENTRAL CONTROLS.

A state which dwarfs its men, in order that they may be more docile instruments in its hands — even for beneficial purposes — will find that with small men no great thing can really be accomplished.
John Stuart Mill
1806-1873

IMPORTANCE OF FREEDOM AND STATES' RIGHTS.

A good society is one which cherishes the highest degree of freedom consistent with order and justice.
Barry Goldwater
1962

UNITED COUNTRIES OF EUROPE COULD BE A NEW SYMBOL OF UNITY AND FREEDOM.

The drafters of the constitution of the new union should avoid strong central controls. History has shown that over-centralization of authority leads to dictatorship and tyranny. Europeans should review carefully the trends in the course of government in the United States of America since its establishment as a nation. The founding fathers of the USA were well aware of the evils of strong central government, and attempted to establish a union where these evils would not exist, or, at least, be held to a minimum. Unfortunately, all too many citizens of the present day (and their political and organization leaders) have overlooked, or have not read carefully, the early documents prepared by our founding fathers. Gradually, the USA is drifting toward greater and greater central control. As this trend proceeds, more and more irresponsibility at the higher levels of government is evident. Individual freedom, and the processes of representative democracy, are gradually diminishing. If the USA is to remain strong and powerful, there will have to be a political reformation—a return to the sound principles of individual freedom and States' rights set forth in the early documents of the country.

Europe has the unique opportunity of creating a new nation where individual freedoms and States' rights can be maintained at high level. The countries of Europe should remain strongly identified as they are today. They should retain their cultural, artistic, linguistic, and, in part, their political heritage. The retention of these would still permit wide cooperation on all problems of mutual concern. Already Europe has demonstrated successful teamwork in the realm of economics and defense. Cooperation in these fields can be advanced and other fields of common concern entered into—but cooperation and unity of action does not mean surrendering all, or even many of the attributes, traditions, and responsibilities of the individual countries or the local governmental units.

The United Countries of Europe could demonstrate a fresh, workable, and vital form of inter-country unity which could be a landmark in the history of nations. Just as the United States of America set a new pattern of governmental organization more than a century and a half ago, so the United Countries of Europe could set a new pattern of national unity in the latter part of the twentieth century. The elements and the environment for this new form of unity exist today in Europe. There yet remains a need only to rally the collective will of the peoples of Europe, and the careful and prayerful guidance of those who will have the responsibility of drafting the documents of unity and government. Just as a group of men, fired with high ideals, a sense of great responsibility, and a fear of God, emerged in America when this nation was struggling toward unity, so there might arise in Europe today a group of leaders who are blessed with the same attributes, high ideals, and sense of noble purpose which filled the hearts of the founders of the USA. May history repeat itself at least in this one respect.

It is of great importance in a republic not only to guard the society against the oppression of its rulers, but to guard one part of the society against the injustice of the other part.

James Madison
1751-1836

We the people of the United States, in Order to form a more perfect Union, establish Justice, insure domestic Tranquility, provide for the common defence, promote the general Welfare, and secure the Blessings of Liberty to ourselves and our posterity, do ordain and establish this Constitution for the United States of America.

Preamble to The Constitution
1787

7

A NEW CAPITAL FOR A NEW NATION

The establishment of a new metropolis as the capital of a new nation will be no easy task. Of the wide range of problems which will be encountered, only a few of those deemed more important are dealt with in this chapter.

A. CENTRALIZATION OF CERTAIN FUNCTIONS, SERVICES, AND FACILITIES

Therefore, with the unmistakable evidence that the countries of Europe are both seeking and achieving a degree of cooperation heretofore unknown, that even greater unity appears to be highly probable in the months and years ahead— even the good possibility of establishing a new nation—is it not timely to give serious consideration to creating a physical focal point for these drives toward unity? Is it not appropriate to think about establishing a new capital?

CERTAIN FUNCTIONS MUST BE CENTRALIZED FOR EFFICIENCY.

For the smooth working of any organization, certain functions must be centralized. This does not mean that all governmental power and authority would be transferred from existing capitals to a new capital. On the contrary, existing European capitals, with their diverse and essential governmental services, would remain as capitals. However, those services and functions essential to the operation of a united nation would naturally be of greater good to all concerned if time and effort in carrying out these services and functions could be minimized. A central location which would facilitate calling together (often on short notice) responsible political and administrative officials would make for a more orderly and effective administrative organization.

Existing, as well as proposed, international cooperative organizations demand staff, equipment, and office space. Many services and functions may tend to overlap or, in part, be duplicated. Dispersion usually results in greater overlapping. Centralization tends to minimize overlapping and duplication. Over and above the centralization of facilities for a smoother staff operation, is the more vital prospect of creating an environment for the easy exchange of ideas between key administrative individuals. The decision-making element of government is of extreme importance. Thus a central area for conferences and various gatherings of executive personnel is most desirable.

The headquarters of existing European international organizations are located in many cities. This scattering has reduced the physical possibility of easy exchange of ideas, and consequently has minimized the effectiveness of each organization. All isolation tends toward separation, lack of understanding and, all too often, mistrust. Effective administration—governmental or otherwise—demands easy communication. Therefore, to minimize travel time of political and administrative leaders, and to achieve the goal of a relatively smooth governmental operation, a central governmental headquarters is reasonable and practical.

A number of countries of Western Europe have been bent on having more international organizations locate their headquarters in their capital cities. There has even been somewhat of a contest, and various inducements have been offered, with the hope of enticing headquarters to each capital. However, the impartial person visiting the present capital cities of Europe would find many things in common: overcrowding of land and most services and facilities; a growing lack of open space; increasing urban population; a severe shortage of adequate housing and great difficulty in relocating families, stores, and other existing features; traffic congestion, which is rapidly worsening; insanitary conditions in many residential and commercial areas; slum and blighted areas which seemingly are expanding rather than being reduced. These, among many other factors, lead one to conclude that no existing capital city, or other large city in Europe, is a fit location for the capital of the new nation.

Politically too, it would be inappropriate to locate the structures and services of the new capital in the capital of any existing country. It is only realistic to recognize the international feelings which exist between the peoples of many European countries. Then there is the problem of prestige in each country and capital city. To move the headquarters of any international organization (public or private) from one capital city to another, would be quite unlikely. Therefore, an attempt at centralization in any existing capital city would immediately create a dilemma. However, centralization of functions in a new area, divorced from any existing capital, and not located within any one existing country, might be acceptable. A new capital in a

PRESENT SCATTERING OF HEAD-QUARTERS A HINDRANCE TO UNITY.

NEW CAPITAL IN CAPITAL DISTRICT POLITICALLY ADVISABLE.

new, free, capital district, in a fairly central area, might be a politically acceptable compromise. This is what is recommended.

B.   LOCATION AND MAGNITUDE OF A NEW CAPITAL FOR EUROPE

PROPOSED SITE FOR NEW CAPITAL.

The author proposes that the new capital district be so located that its territory would not be removed wholly from any one existing country—but rather at the junction of two or more countries, and where urban development does not now exist. With these somewhat basic criteria in mind, there seems only one logical and ideal location for the new capital: at the junction of the three countries of Luxembourg, France, and Germany. At present, the land is primarily used for farming, thus creating no major problem of relocation. The terrain, for the most part, is slightly rolling, permitting rather easy urbanization. The Mosel River and its valley would provide more advantages than problems, and with little trouble, ample water resources would be available for the several demands of a sizable city. Transit links, with transportation lines now used, would be a relatively simple matter. Adjacent forests (of which there are several) could be reserved for recreation and scenic use. The few small farming communities in the area could become the focal points for neighborhoods within the new metropolis.

While the proposed capital would be practically new, from a structural standpoint, there is no reason why certain local and historical landmarks could not be preserved or incorporated in the development to assure ties with history and tradition which are strong in the lives of so many Europeans.

POPULATION OF NEW CAPITAL.

The growth and extent of urbanization of the new capital would be difficult to predict. However, if the growth of other new capital cities is reviewed, and if the growth of present urban areas is analyzed, one might assume that an urban population of from 500,000 to 2,000,000 might obtain by the year 2000.

It is likewise difficult to predict, with any degree of accuracy, what might be the land requirements for these population figures. In contrast to such cities as Luxembourg, Paris, Washington, D.C., the new European capital is conceived as more urban, and with higher density standards. By creating rather large urban sections, predominantly geared to internal pedestrian traffic, large open areas within the urban complex could also be achieved.

The population density of the City of Luxembourg averages about 7,000 persons per square kilometer (18,000 per square mile). The City of Washington, D.C. (within the Federal District) averages about 4,600 persons per square kilometer (12,000 per square mile). Both of these cities are of medium density in contrast to New York or Paris.

The average density for the new capital may logically be from 7,700 persons per square kilometer (20,000 per square mile) to 15,500 persons per square kilometer (40,000 per square mile) and still allow for ample open space within the metropolitan complex, including the central areas. The proposed capital district is visualized with an area of approximately 200 square kilometers (77 square miles). With the junction of the three countries (Luxembourg, France, and Germany) near the center, this would mean a circular area with a diameter of approximately 16 kilometers (9.8 miles). It is further contemplated that a ring of approximately 4 additional kilometers in width around the capital district be designated as within the metropolitan district, and that certain controls for the development of this surrounding district be supervised by the administrative body of the capital district.

Most cities, irrespective of densities, are poorly planned and with little or no calculated balance between built-up areas and open space. Great sections of most cities are misused and haphazardly developed. The reasons for this unfortunate situation are many and complex. One overriding cause, perhaps, has been the very rapid growth in urban areas, with the accompanying lack of planning and direction of physical development. Far less chaos would have resulted had there been organization, through public and private cooperation and action, in the development and redevelopment of many of the present cities.

By preplanning a new city, there is a rare opportunity to avoid many of the blunders and difficulties which are evident in many of today's communities. While mistakes will doubtless be made in building a new capital, and because it is impossible to predict the magnitude of the various forces which will come to play as the cities grow, there is the great advantage of starting fresh. The challenges and opportunities inherent in planning and building a new metropolis are tremendous. Once the concept of a new European capital is accepted, and if wisdom can be brought to bear on every phase of its planning and development, a city might well emerge which would set the pattern for urban development for countless future years. This is now all within grasp. It seems logical, timely, and needed; and by the grace of God, perhaps a new European capital might emerge— a city of no mean reputation, and with a grandeur heretofore unknown. The peoples of Europe can have such a new capital city if they wish it.

DENSITY AND PHYSICAL EXTENT OF NEW CAPITAL.

NEW PREPLANNED CAPITAL COULD AVOID MISTAKES IN PRESENT CITIES.

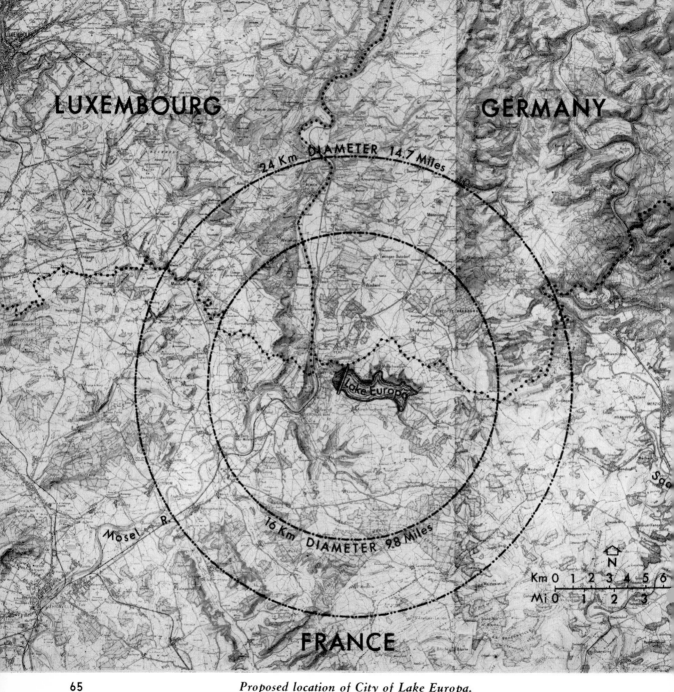

LUXEMBOURG

GERMANY

24 Km DIAMETER 14.7 Miles

Lake Europa

Mosel R.

16 Km DIAMETER 9.8 Miles

N

Km 0 1 2 3 4 5 6
Mi 0 1 2 3

FRANCE

Proposed location of City of Lake Europa.

C. FUNDAMENTALS OF THE PHYSICAL STRUCTURE OF LAKE EUROPA

The physical structure of the new capital is conceived as a composite of rather highly urbanized sections separated by wedges of open spaces. The heart of the capital would center in a "living" lake created by damming up a tributary of the Mosel River almost at the junction of the three countries. The dam and the lake would serve several worthy purposes. The lake would provide an attractive open area available for a variety of sporting and recreational activities. The water would also help to create a delightful lakeside environment for numerous public and semi-public structures. On the rather spacious shores of the lake would be non-governmental facilities: concert halls, cathedrals, churches, large dining establishments (with indoor and outdoor serving areas), park and recreational fields, public recreational clubs, auditoriums, etc.

The basic idea in proposing such land uses is that, by providing an environment where individuals can meet informally, more social, spiritual, and moral achievements might be gained than by allowing the central area to be devoted strictly to governmental and more formal activities. By developing an informal central environment, it is quite possible that even governmental personnel, diplomats, and those participating in any and all official activities, may come to understand each other more fully through informal gatherings. Thus, by creating an attractive convenient central area for informal communication between individuals, it may be that formal discussions in the halls of government and official agencies can be more harmonious and productive.

The lake would have a variety of water sources: the main supplies would come from the two large rivers nearby—the Mosel and the Saar. However, so that the central lake would truly be a symbol of unity, token supplies of water could be brought in (by pipelines) from the major waterways throughout Europe. Thus, the lake would be a constant merging of those streams of the waters which have given life through the centuries to the peoples of Europe—waters of the Rhine, the Rhone, the Seine, the Po, the Elbe, the Loire, the Thames, and the Danube. And the waters of many other rivers could be fed into the pipelines as they focus on "the lake." Token flows from the Baltic and the Mediterranean would be intermingled with the waters of the dozens of rivers and waterways which have had significance in the life and development of the several countries of Europe. Historically, these same waterways have brought the countries through which they have flowed into bonds of unity. Thus, the blending of the waters in the lake of the new capital would be but another somewhat unique illustration of a phenomenon which has actually existed for centuries.

LIVING LAKE GIVES NAME TO NEW CAPITAL—"LAKE EUROPA."

Representing European unity, this new lake would give the name to the new capital—LAKE EUROPA. Among other things, this living lake would be a symbol of the continued unity of Europe, an appropriate contrast to the static monuments built of stone, steel and concrete, which burden the centers of many of the older cities. While the older monuments recall the so-called grandeur of the past—and all too often record military conflicts—the central body of water of Lake Europa would symbolize the future—one devoid of military conflict, where cooperation and harmony would be the aspiration of all Europeans.

NEW DAM HAS MULTI-USES.

The relatively high dam across the Apach Valley just east of the Mosel River, built to create the lake, would in itself offer advantages. Although electric power for the capital region would come from nuclear power generators, the dam would permit an emergency source of hydroelectric power. The top of the dam, as well as the principal bridges over the Mosel River, could be constructed to carry four separate traffic flows on three different levels: the upper level would serve as a roadway for automobiles; the lower level would be a spacious, covered, pedestrian promenade with numerous groups of seats for relaxing and enjoying the wide expanse of attractive scenery over the lake and up and down the Mosel Valley; the center level would carry the monorails on one side and bicycle traffic on the other. At either or both ends of the dam would be ideal locations for exciting and rather exclusive eating establishments, taking full

ATTRACTIONS OF THE LAKE.

advantage of the views. The lake itself would allow for a wide variety of water sports which most Europeans enjoy. Residents and visitors could spend some of their leisure time rowing, sailing, motorboating, swimming, or in the relaxing pastime of observing these activities. Attractive water sports' clubs would grace the shores of the lake, adding that extra sparkle which lifts the spirits of people of all ages. The composite of lake, dam, spillway-waterfall, hydroelectric power plant, the terraced slopes of the Mosel Valley, the variety of lake-side informal activities in their open settings, the numerous streams flowing into the lake carrying waters from all over Europe, would form a total dynamic attraction, wholly appropriate as a focal point for the new capital.

The variety of land uses in Lake Europa would approximate those in the average capital city, although their disposition would be somewhat different. The new metropolis should have a character of urbanity at its best. For centuries Europeans have aspired toward urbanity; they have been, and now are, primarily city dwellers. The new capital would give a fresh opportunity to create the most handsome, attractive, and livable city of which they could dream. By concentrating most structures into a series of pedestrian urban islands, generous open space could be retained in close proximity to all built-up areas.

Insofar as possible, each type and speed of transportation would be provided with its own right-of-way. By minimizing the mixing of various types of traffic, each would be assured easy flow with the least conflict, and the fewest possible accidents. All types of traffic would also move more swiftly as a result of eliminating most intersections at grade. Vehicles of higher speeds using rail or rubber, would be provided with rights-of-way either underground, above ground, or in designated sections of open space between the urban islands. While it would be possible to get about the city rapidly by individual or mass carrier, it is hoped that the entire city would be the delight of the pedestrian, and would be so planned and built that most people would prefer to walk rather than to ride. A fairly complete system of cycle-ways, incorporated throughout the entire metropolitan area (and into adjacent countryside) for the exclusive use of bicycles, is also envisioned. Aside from the pleasure it affords, cycling is known to be one of the healthful forms of physical exercise. With the greater use of the auto, with less physical exercise and consequent muscle softness and attendant physical weakness, lack of health and the loss of the vigor, it is essential that the urban environment encourage all forms of physical fitness. Walking, cycling, rowing, swimming, tennis, and other forms of physical exercise, (indoors and outdoors, and in every season) would be encouraged in the new capital, and every effort would be made to provide the facilities for these year-round healthful activities.

Radiating out from the lake and lake-side, would be a series of wedge-shaped urban complexes, the internal circulation of which would be primarily pedestrian. Alternating between the pedestrian urban islands would be a series of V-shaped open spaces which would provide several features: a physical greenbelt between urban concentrations; open expanses for formal and informal landscaping; outdoor and indoor fields for recreational activities; separate rights-of-way for autos, trains, and other forms of individual and mass transit; rights-of-way for cycles; paths for walking; outdoor classrooms for children to study the wonders of nature; stream beds for the waters piped

GENERAL LAND USE PATTERN OF LAKE EUROPA.

ALL TRAFFIC TO FLOW SMOOTHLY IN NEW CAPITAL.

URBAN ISLANDS AND GREEN WEDGES THROUGHOUT NEW CITY.

RESIDENTIAL STRUCTURES TO HAVE URBAN CHARACTER.

SHELTER FOR GOVERNMENT OFFICES.

to the outskirts of the city from the various waterways of Europe and allowed to flow through these open areas and into the central lake.

Next to open space, the principal land use would be residential. While a variety of residential areas and densities would be planned for, it is suggested that most people would live in some type of multi-family structures. If well designed and properly built, multi-family structures can provide a most satisfactory residential environment. Living balconies would be encouraged for all dwelling units, and full advantage should be taken of all roof-tops and terraces. Urban noise, and other nuisances, would be minimized through a combination of construction requirements of insulation and police regulations regarding sound created by humans, animals, or equipment. A truly urban environment can, and should be, comfortable, convenient, and quiet. There is technical skill and knowledge to assure such an environment. The intelligent application of this skill and knowledge is all that is needed.

While some land uses should be separated from other uses for the benefit of all concerned, it is also possible to integrate many uses which are quite compatible. The planned mixing of related uses can achieve a diversity of activities which would add life to the community. Diversity of uses would also mean greater use of certain fixed facilities which, in turn, is economically desirable, and results in a more logical investment of capital, both private and public. As long as each land use can minimize and contain its own nuisances, these uses may be located in rather close proximity and, in so doing, minimize problems of circulation.

Other than residential, the principal land use would be for activities related directly, or indirectly, to government, intercountry, and international organizations, and to the offices of official representatives of the other nations of the world. Lake Europa, like any capital city, would be the principal seat of the several branches of national government. Here also would be the numerous offices of top government officials, their assistants and staffs. The machinery of any national government is complicated, and it is good administrative practice to house this machinery in related facilities which would enable the "wheels of government" to operate with a minimum of friction.

It would be impossible, and unwise at this time, to indicate the precise location of the various structures which might shelter the wide range of governmental and quasi-governmental activities. However, it is suggested that these important land uses might be located within the many urban islands situated between the green strips which separate these urban complexes, and not in the area adjacent to the lake. A careful study should be undertaken (including an investigation of the land use patterns in other capital cities) to determine the most logical relationship between the location of primary governmental activities and those related activities of secondary and tertiary importance. Likewise, a study should be undertaken to determine desirable relationship of the residential areas housing government officials and employees, to the end that a minimum of time would be lost in getting from home to office. This study should be, primarily, to determine desirable future home-office affinity, and not merely an analysis of what these relationships are in present capital cities. We must assume that the land use and circulation patterns created in Lake Europa would be of such a character as to permit a rather close tie between office and home. The amenities usually associated with residence should be available even in the central sections of the city.

The next major category of land use would be commercial —exchange of goods, services, and ideas—ranging from neighborhood shops to offices of international business organizations. Here again, it is suggested that diversity and convenience be the basic yardsticks for the location of these activities. The wider the influence of these activities, perhaps, the more central should be their location. In all cases, the facilities to house these activities should be contained within the urban islands of the city.

One major group of land uses should be given particular attention—those related to the more informal exchange of ideas, which would include most of the facilities located in the greenbelt surrounding the lake (concert halls, auditoriums, major churches, principal eating establishments, etc.). It is anticipated that Lake Europa will come to be known as a very human city—where people can meet with great ease and where few, if any, barriers are erected to the informal exchange of ideas. In a very real sense, we live in a world of ideas—and the success or failure of governments, industries, all organizations, and the family, depend directly, and continuously, on mutual understanding. The groundwork for most decisions, in both public and private enterprise, is usually laid in informal meetings. Therefore, Lake Europa should be so planned and built that the informal exchange of ideas is encouraged at all times, and at every level of government, private enterprise, and social and religious organizations. All of these activities would be more successful if informal communication could be maintained continuously.

COMMERCIAL LAND USES.

INFORMAL LAND USES AROUND LAKE.

URBAN ISLANDS OF LAKE EUROPA (Example on opposite page)

The new metropolis of Lake Europa is envisioned as a series of concentrated urban areas or "islands" separated by generous greenbelts. Each island would be planned to shelter a variety of compatible uses — residential, commercial, governmental, educational, cultural, recreational, amusement, etc. Through careful planning and adequate insulation, mixed, but related uses could add convenience and life to the community, and almost eliminate wasted hours now required for commuting from home to work. Each urban island would provide a total environment for living, working, and playing.

Traffic would be separated both horizontally and vertically. The ground level of each island, and two or more levels below ground, would be devoted to the automobile — moving and parked. These lower levels would also incorporate areas for storage and utilities, loading and unloading. The first level above the ground level would provide stations for the inter-island monorail trains, and for a variety of shopping and related uses. The next two or three levels would comprise a complex of pedestrian areas, covered and uncovered, free from all vehicular traffic, and incorporating all those uses, facilities, services, and attractions which a city should provide to meet the needs and desires of its inhabitants.

The urban islands of Lake Europa could be an inspiration to planners and builders of cities and metropolitan areas of the future. Each of the components of these urban islands have already been successfully demonstrated. Lake Europa simply provides a new design for these proven elements. The harmonious arrangement of living urban activities, spaces, and structures, could result in a new composition — a "symphony of the city."

71

LAKE EUROPA COULD BE OUT-STANDING EDUCATIONAL AND CULTURAL CENTER.

Lake Europa should become one of the world's most outstanding educational and cultural centers. Here one might find a variety of universities and other institutions of learning, planned as an integral part of the social, political, cultural, religious, and commercial life of the capital. These educational institutions would provide facilities for (and sponsor) programs whereby the people of the community could participate in a wide range of experiences. Education would no longer be conceived as a training period for individuals from the age of 6 to 16 or 26, but rather, a lifelong process of searching for better ways and means of learning and communicating, of understanding and being understood. The primary objective of the education of all ages would be the everlasting pursuit of wisdom and truth. To this end, all educational programs and facilities should be planned. Thus, education (in the broadest sense of the term) would become an integral part of the social and cultural structure of Lake Europa.

NEW CAPITAL A RESEARCH CENTER.

At the same time, the new capital would be an excellent focus for continual experimentation and research in every phase of the learning process. Educators from all parts of the world could come to Lake Europa to observe the new advances in education. Here would be the finest institutes for the training of diplomats, leaders, and top staff at all levels of government. Here, too, would be leading training programs for businessmen and women from many countries. Training institutes would be so organized as not to emphasize the differences between private enterprise and public service, but rather to demonstrate continually by overlapping and interlocking training programs, that there should not be clear distinction between private and public enterprise. This concept of total service to society by both individuals and organizations would be the fundamental principle of all training programs.

A "WORKING LANGUAGE" FOR LAKE EUROPA.

It is advocated that the language of Lake Europa (in and out of school) should be English. This suggestion is based on the simple fact that easy communication is essential to learning, and that, in spite of several inherent difficulties, the English language is gradually becoming the second language for many countries of the world, including most of the countries of Europe. Thus the "working language" of Lake Europa would be English.

The entire language problem of Europe, with its age-old language barriers, could be greatly simplified, and many of the barriers removed, by the widespread acceptance of a common second, or working language in each country. If English were accepted as this second language (which in reality it is in most cases), it would mean that in each country only two languages need be taught—the native language of the country and the second working language, English. If this recommendation were accepted, within one generation each European could communicate with ease with every other European and with most of the people of the world. This simple program could do more toward international understanding (and the vast good which emerges from mutual understanding) than any number of international exchange programs. Actually, through understanding, the entire European population would soon emerge to cultural, economic, and spiritual heights never before realized. Europe could then regain, and retain, its place in world affairs and leadership.

D. FUNDAMENTALS OF THE ADMINISTRATIVE STRUCTURE FOR THE NEW CAPITAL

The creation and growth of a new European metropolis would naturally be accompanied by innumerable, but not insurmountable, problems. In establishing the administrative, as well as the physical and economic, structures, it would be wise to frame these structures so that difficulties might be minimized, and adjustments possible to meet changing demands. If the underlying principles and foundations upon which these several structures are based are humanly, morally, and spiritually sound, the superstructures will likewise have the inherent potentialities of strength and durability.

Any administrative structure should attempt to reflect the will of the people and, at the same time, be as simple as possible, functionally. These two objectives are not necessarily contradictory. It would have to be understood that any form of government, at any level, is just about as good, or as bad, as the people who are in positions of governmental responsibility. Wisdom, honesty, fairness, and integrity, should be attributes of all individuals placed in offices of public trust and service.

Governmental bureaucracy has the unfortunate (but all too accurate) reputation of lacking vision, dynamism, and progressiveness. In large part, this situation is due to the complicated machinery of bureaucracy itself. The more parts a machine has, the greater possibility it has of breakdown or malfunction. It is hoped, therefore, that the governmental machinery of the Lake Europa metropolitan area could be as simple as practicably possible—and yet achieve the goals of good local administration. This should not be an impossible objective to reach—if there is the will to achieve it.

Any administrative structure would have to concern itself with land, buildings, people, services, and the ways and means of maintaining the complexities of a growing and changing

Civilization is the deliberate pursuit of a common ideal. Education is the deliberate attempt to form men in terms of an ideal. A materialistic civilization cannot last. An education that attempts to form men in terms of a materialistic ideal cannot save them of their civilization.

Robert M. Hutchins
1960

CITY GOVERNMENT SHOULD BE OF, BY, AND FOR THE PEOPLE.

ELEMENTS OF THE ADMINISTRATIVE STRUCTURE FOR THE NEW CAPITAL.

metropolis. The local (metropolitan) administrative structure should function as smoothly as possible, uninterrupted, and through time. The administrative structure should be such as to allow for the continual fluctuation and adjustment of the physical environment, with its changing and expanding services, in order to meet the demands of a growing and changing population. Only the fundamental principles of urban development should be maintained, along with the minimum of laws (codes and regulations) to guide that development. Lake Europa should be an outstanding example of the unlimited advantages of the cooperation of public and private enterprise to create and re-create an altogether sound environment—and to maintain it in a wholesome condition through time.

APPLICATION OF PRIVATE ENTER-PRISE TO LOCAL GOVERNMENT.

The administrative structure of the new capital should be patterned after the administrative structure of a business corporation. Such a proposal is not new. One excellent example of a community operating under this type of arrangement is Letchworth, the first Garden City in England, founded in 1903. After almost sixty years of experience, Letchworth, in 1962, is still a very lively, growing, and successful enterprise. It is proposed

LAKE EUROPA DEVELOPMENT AUTHORITY (LEDA).

that this corporation be designated as the Lake Europa Development Authority (LEDA) and that corporate authority be established legally at an early date so that the concept of a new capital might have the continuity desirable from its inception. The composition of the "Board of Directors" of the Authority would be generally (but not exclusively) representative of the several sections of Europe. Those on the Board of Directors would be selected primarily for their ability, broad-mindedness, vision, willingness to work for unity, and their business experience. The Authority should have a 'Chairman' of the Board of Directors and an 'Executive Director.' The first might correspond to a mayor, and the other to a city manager. The Authority might be financed much as any other corporation—from the sale of one or more classifications of stock, upon which interest would be paid to the stockholders. Dividends could be limited to a reasonable return, with surpluses reinvested in facilities and programs for the good of the entire community.

PLANNING AND DEVELOPMENT GUIDED BY LAKE EUROPA DEVELOPMENT COMMISSION.

The development and constant renewal of the physical environment of the metropolitan region of the new capital would be guided by a civic development organization known as the "Lake Europa Development Commission." Members of this commission would be appointed by the Board of Directors of LEDA upon joint recommendation of the local organizations interested in the physical development of the area. During the first years, while the initial development of the capital was taking place, this commission would comprise individuals selected from various parts of Europe. Once the local organizations were well established, the commission members could be recommended by these local bodies. These local organizations might include the chamber of commerce, local chapters of professional groups such as planners, architects, civil engineers, public administrators, etc. The LEDA Board of Directors itself would also recommend possible commission members—outstanding civic-minded, public-respected citizens of the community. Commission members would not represent any particular group in the community or any sub-section of the metropolitan area. They might serve for terms of five years: one-fifth of the total commission appointed every year.

The number of commission members would increase as the population of the new capital grew. During the early years, the commission might number from ten to twenty members. Ultimately, the commission might number between thirty and fifty. Officers of the Board of Directors, and the heads of all operating divisions or departments of LEDA, should be commission members. In all cases, the commission should have a representative executive steering committee to suggest patterns of commission action.

The duties of the commission would be twofold: 1) to recommend broad policies, principles, and appropriate studies related to physical development and redevelopment of the entire metropolitan area; and 2) to review all large-scale, or significant proposals (public and private) for any development or redevelopment in the entire area, or in any given sub-area, in order to recommend possible improvements so that each proposal might benefit alike the community, the developer (or redeveloper), that each proposal might relate as logically as could be determined to a long-range area development concept and improvement program—and in all cases in the public interest.

Commission members should serve without remuneration, with membership limited to two consecutive terms.

Regular meetings of the commission would be held once every three months, with special meetings called by the executive committee. Two-thirds of the membership would constitute a quorum for the executive committee and for the commission.

The full-time staff required to carry out the policies and programs set by the commission would comprise the "Lake Europa Development Department." The Department would consist of four divisions:

1) "Executive Division:" Comprised of five executive staff

Western freedom will not survive just because it is a noble ideal. In the age we live in it will survive if, and I think only if, we can take freedom down with us into the hurly-burly of the competition and conflict and prove that a free society can make itself the good society.

Walter Lippmann
1960

LAKE EUROPA DEVELOPMENT DEPARTMENT.

EXECUTIVE DIVISION.

members appointed by the executive committee of the commission with the approval of the commission. The chairman of the executive division would be an executive director appointed by the executive committee on a rotating basis from the members of the executive division. The executive director would serve as chairman for two years. Members of the executive division would serve at the pleasure of the executive committee.

Remuneration for all members of the executive division would be the same and would be determined by the executive committee.

The duties of the executive division would be to supervise the work of the department as the department serves the commission in performing activities and programs approved by the commission and proposing activities and programs for commission review and action.

GENERAL DEVELOPMENT DIVISION.

2) "General Development Division:" Comprised of adequate staff under the supervision of a division director. The division director to be appointed by the executive division with the approval of the executive committee. The division staff to be appointed by the executive division with the consultation of the division director.

The duties of the general development division would be to carry out general studies on the entire area under the jurisdiction of the commission (and beyond, if thought advisable), and to propose area-wide studies and programs of studies and improvements to the executive division and commission for review and action.

This division would also collaborate with public and private agencies concerned with the development of the area, develop broad patterns of land use and circulation and propose ways and means for achieving (by all avenues of public and private action) these broad patterns. The aforementioned proposals for development would be presented to the executive committee and the commission for review and action.

PERIPHERAL DEVELOPMENT DIVISION.

3) "Peripheral Development Division:" Comprised of adequate staff under the supervision of a division director. Appointment of director and staff to be similar to the general development division.

The responsibility of the peripheral development division would be to collaborate with the general development division on all studies and proposals as they relate to the development of peripheral areas. Collaboration with public and private agencies would follow the same pattern as outlined under the general development division. This division would advise with any governmental agencies concerned with the provision of facilities and services in areas adjacent to the metropolitan capital district. Of special concern would be the location of rail lines, inter-regional highways, airports, regional recreation areas, forest preserves, etc.

4) "Redevelopment Division:" Comprised of adequate staff under the supervision of a division director. Appointment of the director and staff to be similar to the general development division. During the early years of the new capital, the redevelopment division could be relatively small, and its work would be primarily with the existing villages and historical structures in the area. As the city grew, expanded and changed, there would be the constant need to carry out studies of all sections of the community where there was evidence of obsolescence, blight, or lack of adequate maintenance. The division would continually prepare general schemes of improvements and renewal as possible guides for both public and private action; review all renovation, remodeling, redevelopment, and renewal projects in order to suggest ways and means whereby all such actions might be in harmony with the development and redevelopment of the entire community and in the public interest. The division would report its findings and make recommendations to, or through, the executive division and executive committee (and the commission, when advisable) to those responsible for the proposed or actual action involved. The redevelopment division would be primarily an advisory body.

The staffing of the development department would be an all-important problem. Wherever possible, staff members should not be drawn from existing public agencies in other European communities, but rather from the staffs of private business organizations. In all cases, every effort should be made to select individuals who are as forward-looking as possible—with more wisdom than technical knowledge. General training and experience in private enterprise should be given priority over specialized training and experience in governmental agencies. The employment of professional "bureaucrats" with experience in governmental organizations should be avoided whenever possible. While all staff members should respect traditions and cultures of the past, they should in no way "worship" these traditions and cultures. Respect for the past, and worship of the past, are two entirely different qualities. With all of the glories (and shames) of yesteryears, it is essential constantly to remember that the past is simply the prelude to the future.

The spirit of Lake Europa must remain the spirit of youth— a constant striving toward a more attractive and wholesome life in a more attractive and wholesome environment. Lake Europa must ever be a city with a future; and a noble future

REDEVELOPMENT DIVISION.

RECRUITMENT OF STAFF FOR LEDA.

FUTURE OF LAKE EUROPA.

We will never bring disgrace to this our city, by any act of dishonesty or cowardice, nor ever desert our comrades; we will fight for the ideals and sacred things of the city, both alone and with many; we will revere and obey the city laws, and do our best to incite a like respect and reverence in others; we will strive unceasingly to quicken the public's sense of civic duty; that thus in all these ways, we may transmit this city, greater, better, and more beautiful than it was transmitted to us.

The Athenian Pledge

LAKE EUROPA AS A WORLD CENTER.

can be assured if the people of the city will place their community above self. Lake Europa can have a glorious future if its citizens and their leaders take the high road.

A continuing in-service training program for all employees of the new capital would be highly desirable. The learning of new and more efficient ways and means of solving community development problems is always essential. In-service training programs would also provide the vehicle to increase the necessary communication between those individuals who work in related operations, the success of which often depends on communications. Training programs should be both intra- and interdepartmental. There should also be regular seminars and conferences attended by government employees and private citizens. All government employees should be conscious of the fact that they are public servants and, as such, they should have the interest of the citizen in mind. Conferences, seminars, and similar meetings, attended by both government employees and private citizens, would help insure development of the new capital. Communication and cooperation are the foundations of success in all undertakings—and the planning, building, operation, and administration of Lake Europa will be no exception.

E. FUNDAMENTALS OF THE ECONOMIC STRUCTURE FOR THE NEW CAPITAL

To endure through the years, any community must have a healthy economy. To remain continually solvent, a city must possess resources which either do not diminish or which may be replenished. A variety of resources will help insure stability. Resources may be natural and/or human. Products can be tangible and/or intangible. While some communities might rely on salable products for human use or consumption, other communities may prosper on commodities of a more cultural nature. It is anticipated that Lake Europa will be not only a government and educational center but also a generator and reservoir of ideas, which will provide an environment where individuals with creative capacities will feel at home. Lake Europa could soon become one of the world's leading centers for advanced thinking in administration, government, all of the arts, and most of the sciences, education at all levels, and a host of allied fields. A spiritual reawakening could take place also, and the inauguration of a new era of reformation which could result in the rebirth of a deep and lasting conviction in the minds of men to seek a higher plane of spiritual and moral understanding, and a demand for a Christian code of behavior sorely lacking between individuals and nations. All in all, Lake Europa could be a fountainhead of high and mighty movements, setting new and wider horizons for advanced thinking in all fields—of easing the conflicts between men, and of achieving closer associations between man and God.

If even a few of the activities listed above were to become established along with suitable contemporary facilities—all in a healthful and attractive physical environment—the vitality and stability of the local economy would be guaranteed. Each and every one of these functions would serve as a magnet—drawing both men and money to the new capital. And when men of integrity along with financial resources are attracted over a period of time, sound investment and economic stability will be guaranteed.

It is beyond the scope of this volume to detail the ramifications of the economy of the new capital. Our intention here is merely to indicate the logic and soundness of the foundations for a stable economy. For if the foundations of the economic structure are stable, there is an excellent chance that the super-structure of the economy will also be enduring.

F. FUNDAMENTALS OF THE SOCIAL STRUCTURE FOR THE NEW CAPITAL

It has been wisely stated by many authorities that a city is made up, primarily, of the people of the city. The people provide the life and vitality of the community. Lacking people, a city is only a ghost, a lifeless shell. No other single resource is as essential to the well-being of a community as is its people. The combined energy of a free people, guided toward constructive goals for individual and civic betterment, can achieve amazing results. The energies and abilities of the peoples of a capital city constitute a boundless reservoir of ideas which, when freely pooled together, may well generate a vast stream of creative compositions in the arts and sciences. The free peoples of Lake Europa could be an inexhaustible fountainhead of knowledge and wisdom which would benefit not only the new nation, but the peoples of the world. The peoples of the world are yearning for freedom, knowledge, and wisdom. The peoples of Lake Europa, their new capital, their way of life, and their creative works, could be a monumental inspiration to all mankind.

But to remain at their best, the citizens of Lake Europa must remain free—politically, economically, spiritually, and socially. In a free society it is only natural and logical that some individuals will choose to associate with certain other individuals with whom they feel they have something in common. Therefore,

The privilege and responsibility of every citizen in a democratic society is to share in defining the common good as well as in giving service to it. The economic system is a tool for achieving the common good and in a free society is shaped, maintained, and modified by the free choice of the whole community.

William Benton
1944

THE CITY IS THE PEOPLE.

LAKE EUROPA AS A SYMBOL OF A FREE SOCIETY.

Moral and religious education is more important than intellectual education. It is more important to be good than to be intellectual, and it is hard, if not impossible, to be good without being religious.
Robert M. Hutchins
1960

LAKE EUROPA NOT A UTOPIA.

ONLY TWO HURDLES IN WAY OF ACHIEVING NEW CAPITAL.

there will naturally emerge a wide variety of individual and family groupings which must be recognized and accepted. It would be foolhardy to try to mix peoples of widely divergent attitudes, likes or dislikes, philosophies or other differences. People will naturally segregate themselves into intellectual, cultural, economic, professional, and social groupings. It does civic and social harm to all concerned to try forcefully to desegregate such natural groupings. All cities have had, and will continue to have better and poorer sections. By their abilities, talents, and hard work, some people will accumulate more wealth than others. They have every right to spend or save the fruit of the efforts in those ways which they deem proper—just as long as they do not injure others or create a nuisance to their neighbors or their community.

The social structure of Lake Europa will gradually emerge from the social foundations which are laid in the new capital. A free economy based on free enterprise, a free representative political system, and the freedom of religion, will all serve as keystones to a free society. And from a free society may well come a civic order grounded in reasonable laws and understandable justice. Of course Lake Europa, or any other man-made community, will be far from utopia—but with a new start, and a will to achieve a better community, the new capital can be a more wholesome environment in every respect. The opportunities for building a bright and noble capital city will be there —the people of Europe need only to seize them. And if the will is strong enough, and if the vision is bold enough, the new capital can be built.

G.   WAYS AND MEANS OF ACHIEVING THE NEW CAPITAL

Once the concept of a new European capital city has been accepted, there might well be only two major hurdles: 1) acquiring the land; and 2) guiding and regulating the development.

The acquisition of the land for the new capital district could be accomplished by a number of means. Assuming that the governments of France, Germany, and Luxembourg are sympathetic, both to the idea of a new capital and to the proposed location, the required land could be purchased through the application of condemnation procedures. A commission could determine the value of the land, and the owners could be paid a fixed or negotiated price. A good portion of the land—those sections to be developed in later years—could be leased to the present owners to enable continuing productive use. The payments for the land could be drawn from a new fund contributed by governments, foundations, corporations, organizations, and individuals. This land purchase fund could be the first of the general development funds for the new capital.

Lacking inter-governmental support for the new capital in the first few years, the development could proceed as a trusteeship project, pending the time when official governmental action would be taken. A semi-public corporation could be created to carry forward the development idea. The corporation, which might easily take the form of the Lake Europa Development Authority, could draw from a wide variety of financial sources, both public and private. Thus land acquisition, general planning, and initial development, could proceed subject to subsequent official action by governments which might be involved. Once unity was achieved in Europe, and the new capital idea accepted, a transfer of responsibilities, funds, authority, etc., could take place between the interim developers and the new governmental agency which would have the responsibility of developing the new capital. The agency might be the same Lake Europa Development Authority, reorganized to adjust to the new status.

Yet a third alternative would be to create a strictly private development corporation which would undertake land acquisition and development without the cooperation of any government. A Lake Europa Development Corporation could be created, financed by the sale of stock, and operated in much the same way as any other development company. The corporation could agree to transfer its control to a publicly-backed development authority when European unity was achieved, and when the new government would look with favor on designating Lake Europa officially as the capital.

Irrespective of the method of initial development, the author feels that the new metropolis would be a success from the beginning. Once the idea caught fire, the developers, be they public or private, would be faced with the serious problem of controlling the development. Scores of existing international organizations would be anxious to reserve sites for their future headquarters. Foreign countries would clamor for advantageous embassy sites which would give them the prestige they desire. International hotel chains would certainly want sites suitable for their capital city hotels. With the increasing use of the car, motor-hotels would be fashionable in the new capital. Several of the recently conceived interstate motorparks could prosper on the outskirts of the city. Likewise, the corporations which operate major department stores, eating establishments, and other services, would be anxious to locate in the new capital. And so it would be with cultural and educational institutions.

LAKE EUROPA AS A TRUSTEE PROJECT.

LAKE EUROPA AS A PRIVATE DEVELOPMENT PROJECT.

GENERAL PLANNING AT EARLY DATE DESIRABLE.

Many organizations and institutions now located in older and crowded cities might well catch the vision of starting afresh in a new urban environment. The development corporation might be pressed for sites from scores of worthy individuals and organizations, all wanting to become part of the new capital city.

Anticipating such pressure, it is highly desirable to undertake a careful job of general planning at an early date, and certainly before sites were committed to anyone. A general planning and development commission should be set up at an early date to direct all planning and development from the inception of the project. The determination of broad development goals, and the early outlining of the steps necessary to move toward these goals, are essential requisites to guide the logical development of the new metropolis.

NEW CAPITAL AS A TOURIST ATTRACTION DURING CONSTRUCTION.

Once the administrative and economic machinery has been established, the land acquired or otherwise assured, and general plans sufficiently advanced to permit initial construction, Lake Europa would become one of the greatest tourist attractions in all of Europe, if not the world. Those interested, or curious, from all countries would go out of their way to view the building of the new European capital. It would be wise to anticipate such a predictable phenomenon, prepare for, and take full advantage of it. Temporary motels, hostels, camping areas, a variety of dining facilities, and a range of other services, should be planned and built. A carefully worked-out system of pedestrian routes and areas should be provided which would allow visitors to view the construction without interference with it. If properly planned and executed, the entire visitor program with facilities and services could be a profitable venture. Concessions could be let out by the Lake Europa Development Authority, or could be operated by the Authority itself. The promotional and advertising value of such a program in itself would tend to establish a greater assurance of European unity.

It is not difficult to imagine the thrill which thousands of Europeans would get by standing on the very site of the new capital, and witnessing with their own eyes the construction of this new symbol of unity, cooperation, peace, and freedom. Lake Europa would be "their" capital city.

INTERNATIONAL COOPERATION IN HELPING BUILD NEW CAPITAL.

It is entirely within reason to believe that some of the more spectacular elements of the entire project could be accomplished through the cooperation of major industrial organizations. For example, the laying of the hundreds of miles of pipelines to carry the waters of European waterways to "the Lake." Is it not possible that several of the numerous producers of pipes both in Europe and America would count it a worthy international contribution (with the advertising value related thereto) to supply the needed pipe, either at cost, at greatly reduced rates, or even free? Likewise, major petroleum companies of the world, possessing both equipment and skilled workers, could lay the pipe rapidly and efficiently. Perhaps oil companies would also show their willingness to contribute toward the worthy effort by laying the pipe without cost. Inasmuch as the waterlines would be several feet below ground—and once down would not affect the use of the land surface—it is reasonable to assume that the owners of all properties over which the pipe line would run would donate the necessary easements. The major manufacturers of cement and asphalt, and of steel and aluminum, might also contribute to the effort toward unity, peace and freedom. Funds for some of the major buildings—cathedrals, etc.— might come as contributions from individuals and organizations throughout the world.

It is conceivable that several of the large European and American foundations would catch the vision of the positive ramifications of a project of this magnitude and international significance, and make contributions toward the achievement of the new capital. It could be that the contributions of the foundations could initiate the entire program, even before the countries of Europe had established a wholly acceptable pattern of unity. Just as the United Nations came into being before a permanent headquarters was located, so a new capital city could be started before the form of political unity had been determined. Perhaps the easiest method of initiating the project would be to create a Lake Europa Development Company, supported by foundation funds. The project could be started with the mutual understanding that the new capital would be held in trusteeship pending the official establishment of the Lake Europa Development Authority. If the concept were accepted, and the will of the peoples of Europe were to have both unity and a new capital, the ways and means would be found to achieve the new city of Lake Europa.

CONTRIBUTIONS BY FOUNDATIONS FOR BUILDING LAKE EUROPA.

. . . remember that prosperity can be only for the free, and that freedom is the sure possession of those alone who have courage to defend it.

Pericles
469 B. C.

8

INTERNATIONAL APPLICATION AND SIGNIFICANCE OF NEW CONCEPTS FOR THE DEVELOPMENT OF METROPOLITAN COMMUNITIES

RAPID URBANIZATION IN ALL SECTIONS OF WORLD.

Rapidly increasing population in all countries of the world, and the continuing trend of people moving from rural areas to cities, is resulting in forces of urban expansion heretofore unknown. Villages are becoming towns, towns are expanding to cities, and most cities are overflowing into suburban areas and beyond. Even a cursory survey reveals that in most parts of the world, planning for urban expansion is lacking or is far behind the sprawling of people, roads, and structures into the countryside around most centers of population. The forces of urbanization seem to defy both control and guidance. Even worse, there seems to be no let up to expanding population in the foreseeable future.

GROWTH PROBLEMS IN METROPOLITAN COMMUNITIES.

The most severe conditions of overcrowding, congestion, and urban expansion are found in metropolitan communities. Political boundaries, fixed a century or more ago, are now obsolete. Likewise, the systems of taxation and service, usually confined to the legal bounds of the municipality, become ever more unrealistic and inefficient. While population expansion is highly mobile, the ways and means of serving the people are all too rigid. In most countries, the concepts of providing services to urban populations are themselves obsolete and inflexible. It behooves administrators, planners, urban developers, and others concerned with urban development, to devise more adjustable ways and means of guiding and controlling urban expansion. It would be unwise to fight against this trend; it is essential rather to recognize the need for applying all our knowledge and wisdom to meet the challenges of providing urban living and working environments which are wholesome, attractive, livable, and functioning.

We have the tools and the resources to build and rebuild our cities, we have the skills and the workers to handle the job;

the only thing which is really lacking is the will. Then too, all too many people prefer to look back rather than to the future. All too many prefer security to adventure; but progress demands the exploration of new horizons in every field of endeavor. This principle must now be applied to the task of finding new and better ways and means of providing adequately for expanding urban populations. To get the task of exploring under way, it will be essential to assemble both men and equipment. All important are the men, who by training and experience are equipped to be explorers. Unfortunately, all too many men in public office, who believe they are qualified to undertake most tasks related to planning and development, have had their training in the law. By and large, lawyers will not make explorers. By their very training they are taught to look backward, to check cases and decisions for precedents. Exploration does not require precedents, but rather the will to adventure.

One should be fully aware of history and always be ready to profit by the mistakes of others; but first and foremost, there must be the will to venture into uncharted areas and seek out new horizons. If the explorer has the proper training (and is not burdened with the wrong preparation), and has a high degree of faith in his Creator, he should have no question about exploring new horizons.

Progress has always resulted from man's willingness to cut loose from old and traditional ties and strike out into the unknown. The solution to guiding the expanding metropolitan communities will only be found by allowing and encouraging qualified explorers to make new discoveries on the horizons of urban expansion and development.

It is the hope of the author that Lake Europa might serve at least two purposes in the realm of urban research and development. On the one hand, this new metropolis might become a huge laboratory to test the most advanced theories related to metropolitan development. On the other hand, it would be a living demonstration to the peoples of Europe and the world that the building of a new capital can be achieved, and in a relatively short time, if the will of the people is behind the project. Just as the resources of a nation can be marshaled for its defense in time of war, so the resources of Europe are already being marshaled for economic and other forms of international cooperation. These same forces could be put to work in the building of a new capital city, a visual symbol of cooperation and unity, of peace and progress.

The fundamentals outlined in Chapter 7 could be applied to the planning and building of other new communities, and,

BETTER WAYS AND MEANS OF BUILDING AND REBUILDING CITIES MUST BE FOUND.

NEED FOR PIONEERING STUDIES TO SOLVE URBAN PROBLEMS.

LAKE EUROPA COULD BE VAST URBAN RESEARCH LABORATORY.

LAKE EUROPA DEVELOPMENT IDEAS USEFUL ELSEWHERE.

LAKE EUROPA AS DEMONSTRATION PROJECT FOR NEW BUILDING TECHNIQUES.

DEMONSTRATION OF PRINCIPLES OF TRAFFIC SEPARATION.

DEMONSTRATION OF INTEGRATION OF OPEN SPACES THROUGHOUT METROPOLITAN AREA.

FULL USE OF ROOF TOPS.

at the same time, to the renewal of old metropolitan areas. Anticipating continued growth and change in most urban areas, Lake Europa could serve as an inspiration and guide to the leaders in metropolitan regions around the world.

Lake Europa could well be a dramatic demonstration of the successful integration of land and building uses heretofore thought to be incompatible. By the application of performance standards to uses which formerly were associated with nuisances, such as noise and odor, these would-be adverse effects would be so minimized, if not obliterated, that uses once felt to be objectionable would now become compatible neighbors and in many cases result in conveniences and neighborhood assets.

The new capital could also demonstrate the successful application of the principles of traffic separation, both vertically and horizontally. In the open areas of the community, the several traffic flows would be separated by the provision of separate rights-of-way, and with no traffic crossings at grade. This would apply equally to auto, rail, cycle, and pedestrian movements. In the more densely built-up areas—in the so-called urban islands of the community—traffic would be separated vertically. What limited non-pedestrian traffic would be designed into these concentrated areas would be relegated to different levels: a system which would assure safety, convenience, and speed. Every effort would be made to avoid the mixing of different types and speeds of traffic on the same right-of-way. Traffic in the urban island would be primarily pedestrian, and the entire design of these islands would be planned with this in mind. The same principles would be applied to loading and unloading areas, as well as to the parking of cars.

Fully realizing the value of providing open space in urban centers, Lake Europa could demonstrate that open spaces can be provided throughout the metropolitan area, including central sections and, at the same time, permitting the efficient use of all built-up areas. Convenient open space would add to the attractiveness, wholesomeness, economic value, and stability of the entire community.

The new capital could also be designed to take full advantage of most, if not all roof tops. No longer would roofs be unattractive and unused. Gardens, cafes, playcourts, swimming pools, lounging areas and other desirable uses would grace the tops of all buildings. In a very real sense, Lake Europa would be a garden metropolis.

Lake Europa would also demonstrate new concepts of density. Numerous advantages would result in realizing that people move about in a four-dimensional environment, and the number of people in an environment need not have a definite ratio to ground area. In attempting to provide livable and workable density standards, we are dealing with people and their activities in space. This fact must be kept in mind in the planning of all sections of the new community. Perhaps Lake Europa would be a demonstration of the application of "density principles" rather than "density standards." Every attempt would be made to devise new and better ways of providing more wholesome environments for living and working, and, at the same time, sheltering more people on less land. While providing many open spaces, Lake Europa would still be strictly urban—and might well set standards for other urban areas to follow.

In harmony with the density and traffic principles noted above, it is suggested that new concepts be applied to the housing of embassies and similar headquarters and residences of government officials. Rather than to locate offices and residences of ambassadors on large tracts of land in various sections of the capital, it is proposed that both offices and residences of such officials be sheltered in multi-storied structures in central areas. While privacy would be assured to all activities, the staff would have the great advantage of convenience; and through closer association, both formally and informally, many of the problems usually developing from lack of easy communication could be minimized. If top officers and their staffs could mingle together and perhaps dine and play together more often, some of the problems which develop between more isolated groups would be minimized. It is quite possible that by building an environment wherein the roots of friendly relations mature more readily, more cordial human relations would develop. If this were the case, Lake Europa would indeed be worth all of the time and effort and expense which would go into the planning and building of the new capital. This same concept could be applied with equally positive results to the grouping of headquarters of organizations in cities throughout the world. If urban environments would provide for easier communication in friendly and informal atmospheres, perhaps many of our international tensions and difficulties would diminish.

Lake Europa will be far from a utopia. It is conceived as a purely human metropolis: planned and built by the minds and hands of men. The planning and building process will not be without difficulties and there will be many conflicting opinions in every phase of the work. However, if the concept is deemed to be sound, logical, and timely, and if the peoples of Europe have the will to strive toward unity, peace, and freedom, they may also catch the vision of the many benefits accruing to them

LAKE EUROPA AS DEMONSTRATION OF NEW CONCEPTS OF URBAN DENSITY.

DEMONSTRATION OF GROUPING OFFICES AND RESIDENCES IN HIGH-RISE BUILDINGS.

LAKE EUROPA COULD BE A METROPOLIS IN HUMAN SCALE—A SYMBOL OF A FREE AND UNITED EUROPE.

88

as individuals and as a united people, in the building of a new symbol of their will to cooperate and their desire to be free. Such a symbol could be their new capital—the City of Lake Europa.

A purpose is not the same thing as a wish. Or a dream. Or even a mission. But one fundamental purpose of a democracy is the exercise of reasoned choice, the conscious shaping of events. Even setbacks would be more meaningful if—to use Hamilton's phraseT instead of being ruled by "accident," we could govern ourselves by "reflection and choice." If the hard problems of our time stir us to more reflective choice, then they will have helped us fulfill one important purpose of a democratic society.

Albert Wohlstetter
1960

GLOSSARY OF SELECTED INTERNATIONAL ORGANIZATIONS

Note: The organizations listed below are but a sampling of the hundreds of international bodies having headquarters in Europe. The vast majority are mostly or wholly European, and with few exceptions have been founded since the end of World War II. This inventory of international groups has been taken primarily from five sources.[1] Each listing gives the common abbreviation, the full name of the organization, headquarters' location, founding date, and type of membership.

ACUSE	Action Committee for a United States of Europe Paris; 1955; Individuals in 6 European countries.
AEDE	European Association of Teachers Paris; 1956; National associations of teachers in 7 European countries.
AEF	European Center for Federalist Action Paris; 1956; National movements in 7 European countries.
AIT	International Touring Alliance Geneva; 1893; National organizations in 76 countries.

ATA	Atlantic Treaty Association
	    London, 1954; Voluntary national organizations in 10 European countries,
	        Canada and the USA.

BENELUX	Benelux Economic Union Brussels; 1958; Governments of Belgium, Netherlands, and Luxembourg.
BIPM	International Bureau of Weights and Measures Sevres (France); 1875; Governments of 36 countries.
BIS	Bank of International Settlements Basle; 1930; European central banks.
CCR	Central Commission for the Navigation of the Rhine Strasbourg; 1815; Governments of 6 European countries and the USA.
CE	Council of Europe Strasbourg; 1949; Governments of 16 European countries.

CEA	European Confederation of Agriculture
	    Brugg/Aargau (Switzerland); 1948; Professional groups, institutions, and in-
	        dividuals in 19 countries, mostly European.

CEAA	Congress of European American Associations Antwerp; 1951; Associations in 16 European countries.
CERN	European Organization of Nuclear Research Geneva; 1954; Governments of 13 European countries.

[1]"Europa Year Book 1962, The," Vol. I (London: Europa Publications, Ltd., 1962) 1262 pp.; "International Organizations" (Amsterdam: J. H. De Bussy, 1960) 99 pp; Kenneth Lindsay, "European Assemblies: The Experimental Period, 1949-1959" (London: Stevens & Sons, Ltd., 1960) 267 pp.; A. H. Robertson, "European Institutions" (London: Stevens & Sons, Ltd., 1959) 372 pp.; "Yearbook of International Organizations" 7th Edition, 1958-59 (Brussels: Union of International Associations, 1958) 1269 pp.

CIEC	International Commission on Civil Status
	The Hague; 1950; Governments of 7 European countries.
CJ	Court of Justice (of the European Community)
	(No headquarters as yet); 1957; Governments of 7 European countries.
CODIP	The Hague Conference on Private International Law
	The Hague; 1955; Governments of 17 European countries, the UN, and Japan.
COIRT	Central Office for International Railway Transport
	Bern; 1890; Railways of 25 European countries.
CPE	Congress of the People of Europe
	Turin (Italy); 1956; Committees in 6 European countries.
EAPA	European Alliance of Press Agencies
	Brussels; 1957; Press Agencies in 16 European countries.
EBF	European Baptist Federation
	London; 1950; Baptist unions in 21 European countries.
EBU	European Broadcasting Union
	Geneva; 1950; 48 members, including 27 from European countries. Sponsor of EUROVISION.
ECC	European Cultural Centre
	Geneva; 1950; Five European cultural bodies.
ECE	Economic Commission for Europe
	Geneva; 1947; Governments of 29 countries, mostly European.
ECMT	European Conference of Ministers of Transport
	Paris; 1953; Governments of 17 European countries.
ECPS	European Centre for Population Studies
	Paris; 1953; Representatives in 14 European countries.
ECSC	European Coal and Steel Community
	Luxembourg; 1952; Governments of European countries, plus agreements with two other countries.
EEC	European Economic Community
	Brussels; 1958; Governments of 6 European countries. (The "Inner Six" or "Common Market" countries.)
EFC	European Forestry Commission
	Rome; 1948; Governments of 21 European countries and Israel.
EFTA	European Free Trade Association
	Geneva; 1959; Governments of 7 European countries (the "Outer Seven").
EIB	European Investments Bank
	Brussels; 1957; Governments of 6 European countries.
ELEC	European League for Economic Cooperation
	Brussels; 1946; National Committees in 9 European countries.
ELMH	European League for Mental Hygiene
	Paris; 1951; National leagues in 16 European countries.
EM	European Movement
	Brussels; 1947; National councils in 15 European countries.
EMA	European Monetary Agreement
	Paris; 1958; Governments of 17 European countries.

EMCC	European Municipal Credit Community
	Turin (Italy); 1954; Founder members and national sections in 7 European countries.
EPA	European Productivity Agency
	Paris; 1953; Governments of 17 European countries.
EPARA	European Parliamentary Assembly
	Luxembourg; 1958; Individuals nominated by Parliaments in 6 European countries.
EPG	European Press Group
	London; 1956; 12 newspapers in 10 European countries.
EPPO	European and Mediterranean Plant Protection Organization
	Paris; 1951; Governments of 30 countries in Europe and adjacent Mediterranean areas.
ERO	European Regional Organization of the ICFTU
	Brussels; 1950; 19 national trade unions in 16 European countries.
ESC	Economic and Social Committee
	Brussels; 1957; Individuals representing 6 European countries.
ESRC	European Society for Rural Sociology
	Bonn; 1957; Individuals, institutions, and associations in 14 European countries.
EUF	European Union of Federalists
	Paris; 1946; National organizations in 8 European countries.
EURAILPASS	Sponsored by Plenary Conference for Eurailpass (PCE)
EURATOM	European Atomic Energy Community
	Brussels; 1958; Governments of 6 European countries.
EUROFIMA	European Company for the Financing of Railway Rolling Stock
	Basle; 1955; National railway administrations of 16 European countries.
EUROVISION	Sponsored by European Broadcasting Union (EBU)
EUW	European Union of Women
	Vienna; 1955; National sections in 7 European countries.
EYC	European Youth Campaign
	Paris; 1951; National secretariats or correspondents in 15 European countries.
FAIB	Federation of International Associations Established in Belgium
	Brussels; 1949; 54 international associations established in Belgium.
FAO	Food and Agriculture Organization
	Rome; 1945; A specialized agency of the United Nations, comprising (in 1960) 78 member nations and 9 associate members.
FCTU	Federation of Christian Trade Unions in the ECSC
	Luxembourg; 1955; 26 national confederations and federations in 5 European member countries.
FID	International Federation of Documentation
	The Hague; 1895; National committees in 25 countries, and individual or collective associate members in 34 countries.
FIIG	Federation of Semi-Official and Private International Institutions Established in Geneva
	Geneva; 1929; 36 international organizations established in Geneva.

GATT	General Agreement on Tariffs and Trade
	Geneva; 1947; Agreement accepted by 37 governments with 6 others taking part.
IAEA	International Atomic Energy Agency
	Vienna; 1957; Governments of 70 countries.
IBSTP	International Bureau for the Supression of Traffic in Persons
	London; 1889; 7 appointed members together with delegates of national committees in 29 countries.
ICA	International Cooperative Alliance
	London; 1895; 480,000 cooperative societies in 48 countries.
ICC	International Chamber of Commerce
	Paris; 1919; Federation of 41 national sections in 65 countries.
ICEM	Intergovernmental Committee for European Migration
	Geneva; 1951; Governments of 29 countries, including 14 European nations.
ICES	International Council for the Exploration of the Sea
	Charlottenlund (Denmark); 1902; Governments of 16 European countries.
ICFPW	International Confederation of Former Prisoners of War
	Paris; 1949; Six national federations in 5 European countries.
ICFTU	International Confederation of Free Trade Unions
	Brussels; 1949; National trade unions with members in 102 countries.
ICPO	International Criminal Police Organization (INTERPOL)
	Paris; 1923; Official police bodies in 63 countries.
ICRC	International Committee of the Red Cross
	Geneva; 1863; International Committee of the Red Cross; League of Red Cross Societies; and National Red Cross Societies.
ICSU	International Council of Scientific Unions
	The Hague; 1931; Scientific academies, national research councils, associations of institutions or governments in 43 countries.
ICW	International Commission on Whaling
	London; 1946; Governments of 16 countries.
IFCTU	International Federation of Christian Trade Unions
	Brussels; 1920; National trade union confederations in 56 countries.
IFHP	International Federation for Housing and Planning
	The Hague; 1913; Organizations, agencies, bodies, institutions, and individuals in 43 countries.
IFL	International Friendship League
	London; 1931 National sections in 11 European countries.
IFRM	International Federation for the Rights of Man
	Paris; 1922; Affiliated sections in 6 European countries.
IFTA	International Federation of Travel Agencies
	Brussels; 1919; National groups, firms, and individuals in 70 countries.
IHA	International Hotel Association
	Paris; 1946; National hotel associations and individuals in 80 countries.
IIB	International Patent Institute
	The Hague; 1947; Governments of 6 European countries and Morocco and Tunisia.

ILO	International Labor Organization Geneva; 1919; Governments of 83 countries.
ILRS	International League of Religious Socialists Bentveld (Netherlands); 1922; Associations in 9 European countries.
IMCO	Inter-Governmental Maritime Consultative Organization London; 1958; Governments of 39 countries.
IPI	International Press Institute Zurich; 1951; Newspaper editors in 45 countries.
IPU	Inter-Parliamentary Union Geneva; 1889; National groups in 58 countries.
IRU	International Road Transport Union Geneva; 1948; Transport organizations in 17 European countries with associate members in 5 other countries.
ISI	International Statistical Institute The Hague; 1885; 5 international organizations, 15 national affiliated organizations, and 410 individuals.
ISO	International Organization for Standardization Geneva; 1946; Standard bodies in 44 countries.
ITU	International Telecommunication Union Geneva; 1865; Governments of 101 countries.
IUPLAW	International Union for the Protection of Literary and Artistic Works Geneva; 1886; Governments of 45 countries.
MFE	European Federalist Movement Paris; 1946; Organizations in 8 European countries.
NATO	North Atlantic Treaty Organization Paris; 1949; Governments of 15 countries, including 13 European countries.
NC	Nordic Council Copenhagen; 1952; Governments of 5 Scandinavian countries.
OECD	Organization for Economic Cooperation and Development Paris; 1961; Governments of 18 European countries. Canada and the USA are associate members.
PCE	Plenary Conference for Eurailpass Paris; 1958; National railways of 13 continental European countries. Current conference chairmanship held by French National Railways. Sponsor of EURAILPASS.
PCEM	Parliamentary Council of the European Movement Brussels; 1952; Parliamentary groups in 15 European countries.
PCPDRNWE	Permanent Conference for Planned Development of Regions in North West Europe Liege; 1955; Individuals and representatives of regional institutes in 5 European countries.
PEN	International Pen London; 1921; Autonomous centers in 55 countries with 7000 members.
SCAR	Scandinavian Council for Applied Research Stockholm; 1947; Chairmen and secretaries of national technical academies and research councils in 5 Scandinavian countries.

SPC   Scandinavian Patent Committee
                     Copenhagen; 1955; Governments of 4 Scandinavian countries.

SMUSE   Socialist Movement for the United States of Europe
                     Paris; 1947; National selections in 10 European countries.

TAB   Technical Assistance Board
                     Geneva; 1949; Executive heads of the UN and of 8 of the specialized agencies of the UN.

UIPPI   International Union for the Protection of Industrial Property
                     Geneva; 1883; Governments of 48 countries.

UIR   International Union of Railways
                     Paris; 1922; Railway administrations in 39 countries.

UNESCO   United Nations Educational, Scientific and Cultural Organization
                     Paris; 1946; Governments of 80 countries, with 4 other countries having associate membership (as of 1958).

UNHCR   Office of the United Nations High Commissioner for Refugees
                     Geneva; 1951; Governments of 25 countries have ratified the convention relating to the status of refugees (as of 1960), 17 of these countries being European.

UPU   Universal Postal Union
                     Bern; 1874; Governments of 98 countries.

UT   International Conference for Promoting Technical Uniformity on Railways
                     Bern; 1882; Railway organizations in 18 European countries.

WATA   World Association of Travel Agencies
                     Geneva; 1949; 208 individual members and correspondents in 70 countries.

WCC   World Council of Churches
                     Geneva; 1948; A fellowship of 173 (as of 1960) denominations in 53 countries. Roman Catholic Church is not included.

WEU   Western European Union
                     London; 1955; Governments of 7 European countries.

WFTU   World Federation of Trade Unions
                     Prague; 1945; More than 100 million workers in most countries of the world. Workers' organizations in 80 countries were represented at the 1957 Congress of WFTU.

WHO   World Health Organization
                     Geneva; 1948; Governments of 101 countries.

WMO   World Meteorological Organization
                     Geneva; 1947; Governments of 77 countries and 25 territories or groups of territories.

APPENDIX B

BRIEF SKETCH OF THE INQUISITION —

4th to the 20th CENTURY

The institution of the Inquisition, as advocated by the "Holy Office" of the Roman Catholic Church, spans many centuries. It has been pursued more drastically at different times and in different areas during the past fifteen centuries. Basically, the Roman Church felt justified in inflicting suffering and torture on any human beings who were judged (by the Church authorities) to be unbelievers or heretics. Their property, both real and personal, was often confiscated. The extent of the inhuman and often sadistic torture applied to the innocent in trying to extract confessions was a matter to be determined by the local church officials, or by the local civil authorities with the blessings of the Church. Lea suggests that the Inquisition divides itself naturally into two parts: pre- and post-Reformation.[1]

The first records of official persecution by Roman Catholic authorities date back to the times of Valentinian I (321-375) and Theodosius I (346-395).[2] From this period forward there is abundant evidence that Church action against so-called unbelievers became more regular, more extensive, and more cruel, often unto death.

The practice of inflicting torture on unbelievers gained momentum in the 11th century, and was especially severe and widespread in the 12th and 13th centuries. Accusation of heresy could be made by almost anyone, and the accused had practically no recourse. The Dominican, Bernard Guy (1261-1331), one of the most complete exponents of the theory of the Inquisition, admits that the procedure was secret and, in the highest degree, arbitrary. All of the accused were presumed to be guilty —the judge being at the same time the accuser. Severe torture seemed to be more widely practiced in the Latin countries. Dr. J. M. Carroll, in his little booklet "The Trail of Blood,"[3] states that during the twelve centuries beginning with the year A.D. 426, about 50 million Christians died martyr deaths at the hands of the Roman Catholics. However, it was perhaps the widespread revolt against both the atrocities of the Inquisition and

---

[1] Henry Charles Lea, "A History of the Inquisition of the Middle Ages" (New York: Russell & Russell, 1958), Vol. I, Preface.

[2] "The Encyclopaedia Britannica," Fourteenth Edition (London: The Encyclopaedia Company, Ltd., 1938), Vol. 12, p. 377.

[3] J. M. Carroll, "The Trail of Blood," Lexington, Kentucky: Ashland Avenue Baptist Church, 1931, 55 pp.

the corrupt practices of the Church in selling indulgences which gave impetus to the Reformation in Northern Germany.

The spread of the Reformation during the 16th and 17th centuries brought forth new and vicious waves of merciless torture for those who dared question the dictates of the Roman Church, and punishment by burning at the stake was commonplace in many areas.

A fanatical regional phase of this institution of torture had its headquarters in Madrid, and is generally known as the "Spanish Inquisition." The "Holy Inquisition" in Spain originated during the papacy of Innocent III (1198-1216)[4] and its inhuman administration was condoned (even urged) by the succeeding popes, Sixtus IV, Alexander VI, Innocent VIII, Julius II, and later by the popes of the 16th century.[5]

The Spanish Inquisition was doubly harsh in that its torturous practices were advocated jointly by the Roman Catholic Church, the Spanish Crown (a Catholic) and the royal henchmen. Indeed, it often appeared as if these three sponsors would vie in trying to outdo each other in severity of persecution and torture.

During the 16th and 17th centuries, the Inquisition in Spain was directed against Protestantism. Burning of Lutherans was common, even though they were not considered backsliders.[6]

With the extension of the Spanish Colonial Empire, the Inquisition spread throughout Latin America almost contemporaneously with the Catholic faith. Ferdinand V (called the Catholic) (1452-1516) decreed the establishment of the Inquisition in America. The administration of the Spanish Inquisition in the New World was directly responsible for the merciless slaughter of thousands of native American aborigines. Entire tribes and nations of American Indians were murdered because of their unwillingness to accept the Roman Catholic faith.

Nor is the Spanish Inquisition in Latin America a matter of history. In this year of 1962 A.D., the persecution of Protestants in most Latin American countries continues. This "20th century version of the Inquisition" has been especially violent in Colombia.[7] Although the Roman Catholic Press consistently denies that Protestants have been persecuted in Colombia, there is abundant evidence, well documented, including the United States Embassy in Bogota. The Evangelical Confederation of Colombia,

---

[4]William S. Roeder, Editor, "Dictionary of European History" (New York: Philosophical Library, 1954), p. 144.
[5]Encyclopaedia Britannica, *op. cit.*, Vol. 12, pp. 381-382.
[6]*Ibid.*, Vol. 12, p. 383.
[7]Clyde W. Taylor, "The Fate of Protestants in Colombia," "Christianity Today," Vol. II, No. 2, October 28, 1957, pp. 11-13, and Vol. II, No. 3, November 11, 1957, pp. 15-17.

an interdenominational organization of Protestant missionary agencies in Colombia, has published scores of firsthand accounts of the cruelest forms of persecution, even to the extent of extreme torture and death.[8] An authenticated record[9] of thirteen years' (1947-1960) religious persecution in Colombia shows an appalling total of 116 Protestant Christians martyred because of their religious faith, 66 Protestant churches and chapels destroyed by fire or dynamite, and over 200 Protestant day schools closed. The accounts show that Roman Catholic priests usually take the leading roles in these inhumane and uncivilized acts. And they are often aided and abetted by the so-called local "law-enforcing" agencies which are dominated by the Catholic hierarchy. Nor is this situation likely to change in the near future, not as long as the government of Colombia does not revoke two treaties made with the Vatican—the "Concordat" in 1887, and the "Mission Treaty" in 1953; and the "circular orders" issued by the Colombian Minister of Government under the military dictatorship of 1953-1957. All too many officials of Latin American governments are dominated by the Roman Catholic Church. Thus when direct violence, persecution and destruction fail, pseudo-legal means may be sought to suppress Protestantism.

It is likewise common knowledge that those who try to teach any Protestant doctrine, or those who try to live by such beliefs in countries dominated by the Roman Catholic Church, like Spain[10] and Ireland,[11] do so often at great risk to life and property. Nor are the conditions in Italy, France and Portugal much better.

Thus, from the fourth to the twentieth century, persecution of non-Catholics by Roman Catholic leaders and followers has been almost continuous. Seemingly, one of the four fundamental freedoms to which all men who cherish freedom aspire—the freedom of every person to worship God in his own way—is not to be found in the vocabulary of the Roman Catholic Church. It is a paradox that the Catholic Church, which claims to adhere to the teachings of Christ, is so violently opposed to those who try to spread the Word of God.

---

[8]Bulletins of the Evangelical Confederation of Colombia (especially Bulletins Numbers 64, 65, 67, 68, and 69) published from August 1960 to 1961, by the Office of Information and Public Relations, Evangelical Confederation of Colombia, Barranquilla, Colombia.

[9]James E. Goff, "What's Behind the Persecution in Colombia?" Latin American Evangelist, May - June 1961, pp. 2-5.

[10]Herbert L. Matthews, "The Yoke and the Arrow: A Report on Spain" (New York: George Braziller, Inc., 1957), pp. 138-165.

[11]Paul Blanshard, "The Irish and Catholic Power: An American Interpretation" (Boston: The Beacon Press, 1953), 375 pp.

However, the Roman Catholic Church is not alone in this guilt of persecution. Many of the religious groups which emerged after the beginning of the Reformation became dogmatic and dealt harshly with any who held contrary to their beliefs. History shows that whenever any religious body is espoused by a government, and is acclaimed to be "the established church," persecution has been most severe. Therefore, if men are to achieve freedom in the fullest sense of the term, including "religious freedom," it is essential that church and state be separated, and be kept separate.

And you will know the truth and the truth will set you free.
John 8:32

UNITED STATES OF EUROPE — HOPE OF THE WEST

Step by step, the nations of Western Europe are creating a force which the communists are unable to stop: the massive power of economic unity.

From "Saturday Review," as condensed in the February 1962 "Reader's Digest."

By Roscoe Drummond

Washington columnist, New York Herald Tribune Syndicate

While the shape of things to come is not yet fully in focus, the West is at the point of bringing to fruition a vast and galvanic enterprise capable of changing the whole face of the cold war.

This is not a new military alliance designed to win a war. It is a new economic and political alliance capable of winning the peace.

I venture to state that within the remaining years of this decade we will witness a coherent, fully functioning United States of Europe—one that will be producing an annual gross national product probably greater than that of the United States.

Along with the U.S.A., the new alliance will so clearly demonstrate the vigor of its competitive enterprise, free-market, pro-consumer economy that communism will look to more and more people like the wave of the past.

Is this wishful thinking? I think not. There is solid evidence to support this judgment. We have had our minds so fixed on the crises the communists have created—from Vietnam to Berlin—that we have failed to see the pattern of positive events developing under our very eyes.

The fact is that the burgeoning Common Market is bringing European political unification steadily nearer.

This international trading area—embracing the six nations of France, West Germany, Italy, the Netherlands, Belgium and Luxembourg in a single economic union and serving 170 million European consumers—is proving to be an economic success beyond all expectations of its founders.

The British government, in a revolutionary decision last fall, made application to join the six countries, though this would cause Britain to alter her ties with the Commonwealth, abandon her historic aloofness from the Continent and dilute some of her own sovereignty. Norway, Denmark and Eire will almost certainly follow suit. This will create a European Economic Federation of ten nations and 250 million people whose goods, farm products and workers will soon be able to move as freely across national frontiers as ours move across state borders in the United States.

These events are capable of changing the whole face of the cold war. With British participation, the European Common Market can collectively share the leadership of the free world with the United States. This combination can constitute a political and economic power center which the communists cannot match in this century—if ever.

Both the British and the men in the Kremlin know quite well that a momentous turn in events is in the making. Prime Minister Harold Macmillan put it in muted phrases when he made the announcement in the House of Commons

[1]First published in "Saturday Review" of November 4, 1961. Reprinted here with the permission of Saturday Review, Inc., and The Reader's Digest Association, Inc.

last July 31. On the eve of the necessary negotiations, he did not wish to stir unnecessary controversy or premature hopes. But Desmond Don-
nelly, a leading intellectual in the Labor Party,
did not hesitate to put the wider meaning in
these words:

"The Prime Minister's statement is a clear
indication that Britain's frontier is not at Dover
but at the Brandenburg Gate."

Khrushchev knew it, too. He immediately
branded the British decision as a "capitulation"
to the greedy economic forces of the "City,"
thus hoping to divide British opinion and stir
sufficient Parliamentary opposition to reject the
government's decision.

The Soviet leader realizes that what the members of a ten-nation European Common Market
can do in "behalf of each other" will be a far
greater deterrent to Soviet designs than anything they or others are likely to do against the
Soviet Union. This is why the Common Market
is such a powerful weapon in the cold war. It is
no military alliance and hence cannot be effectively countered—just as the Marshall Plan could
not be effectively countered by the Soviets. This
infuriates and alarms Khrushchev, who sees the
Common Market making tremendous headway
while he is helpless to resist it.

How successful has the Common Market
become since it was brought into being by the
six nations in 1958?

During the brief four years all of the member
countries have achieved a rate of sustained
economic growth never before experienced in
the history of Europe. Workers and employers,
industry and labor, consumers and producers are
sharing in an economic recovery and in a prosperity more rapid and more sustained than any-
where else in the world.

The gross national product of the European
Community rose seven percent in 1960 over
1959 in terms of constant prices and climbed
at a five-percent rate during 1961. Industrial
production went up 12 percent in 1960 and has
expanded 25 percent in three years.

Because of this dynamic growth, the Common
Market has been able to move far more rapidly
than originally planned, in scaling down tariffs
and other trade barriers within the six-nation
area. By the end of 1961 all quota restrictions
on trade in industrial goods between the six
countries had been abolished—eight years
ahead of schedule.

The opening of the frontiers to competition
has brought benefits far greater than the community's most ardent advocates believed attain-
able. Most leaders of industry in Western Europe
were at first either hostile or skeptical toward
the Common Market enterprise. But now the
cartel-minded Europeans have come almost full
circle in their attitude. They are finding that the
rewards of producing for a competitive market
of 170 million consumers are far greater than
they ever enjoyed in the prewar years. Proof
of this is that business has been tending more
and more to draw up development and distribution networks on the scale of the Common Market in full operation.

For the past five years Britain, which must sell
abroad in order to buy abroad, has seen its
share of the world's exports drop four percent
while the Common Market countries' share of
world exports climbed 20 percent. This is why
the British government has now made the pain-
ful but epochal decision to become a full-
fledged partner in the European Common
Market.

Winston Churchill, in his famous speech at
Zurich in September 1946, when so few could
see beyond the wreckage and impoverishment
of the war, said:

Over wide areas a vast quivering mass of
tormented, hungry, careworn and bewildered human beings gaze at the ruins of their
cities and homes, and scan the dark horizon
for the approach of some new peril. Among
the victors there is a babel of jarring voices,
among the vanquished the sullen silence of
despair. Yet all the while there is a remedy
which would as if by a miracle transform

the whole scene. It is to re-create the European family, or as much of it as we can, and provide it with a structure under which it can dwell in peace, in safety and in freedom. We must build a kind of United States of Europe.

It is being built.

Even today there is an immediate point at which the expanding European Community can play a crucial part in arresting Soviet ambition. That point is Germany. Premier Khrushchev's goal is not merely to neutralize Berlin. His larger goal is to detach all of Germany from its ties to the West and to reduce NATO to impotence.

By annexing East Berlin to East Germany and East Germany to its European satellite empire, the Kremlin has snuffed out all prospect of German unification. Khrushchev can now say to Bonn: "You have misplaced your trust in your Western allies. They cannot give you a united nation. We alone can give you a united Germany."

An economically and politically disunited Western Europe would sorely tempt many Germans to reach for the Soviet bait, with calamitous consequences for the whole Western position. An economically and politically united Western Europe, as is now coming to fruition, will make Khrushchev's offer a bleak and unattractive thing.

But there is more to be done. The urgent question is: What next?

Surely we in the United States are not going to neglect to do our part in carrying forward the tremendous momentum of the European Community. We are already using the new Atlantic economic organization, the Organization for Economic Cooperation and Development, in which we are now a member along with Canada and the European nations. This is evidence of our awareness of the interdependence between Europe and North America.

The need now is for the United States to go much further toward the expansion of the European-British Community into an Atlantic Community. It is time to get ready to take this step.

The father of today's united Europe, Jean Monnet, now president of the Action Committee for the United States of Europe, has put it this way: "Just as the United States in its early days found it necessary to unite, just as Europe is now in the process of uniting, so the West must move toward an Atlantic concert of nations. This is not an end in itself. It is the beginning on the road to the more orderly world we must have to escape destruction."

At its present galvanic stage the European-British Community will be capable of arresting the adverse trend of the cold war. An Atlantic Community embracing Europe, the United States and Canada will be capable of "reversing" that trend—by creating a united and permanent preponderance, a dynamic which would be irresistible to other nations.

Representatives of old and new world cooperate in building "altar" marking the site of "Lake Europa." Mr. Roger Krieps, of the Luxembourg newspaper *d'Letzeburger Land* and Prof. Miller lay first stones of monument near the Mosel River at the junction of the countries of Luxembourg, France, and Germany. 8 September 1961.

Prof. Miller addressing group at "pre-dedication ceremony" at site of proposed new European capital, "Lake Europa." 8 September 1961.

European and American pledge cooperation in pursuit of European unity. M. Pierre Wallerich, a resident in the area of the proposed European capital of "Lake Europa" and Prof. Miller exchange greetings at conclusion of "pre-dedication ceremony" at site of proposed metropolis. 8 September 1961.

(*Photos by Tony Krier*)

APPENDIX D

REMARKS BY PROF. J. MARSHALL MILLER

on the occasion of the designation and "pre-dedication" of the site for LAKE EUROPA: A NEW CAPITAL FOR A UNITED EUROPE, 8 September 1961, in the Valley of the Mosel River, near the junction of Luxembourg, France, and Germany.

We are assembled here today on an occasion which may have great significance in the years ahead. Only God knows what may emerge from the seeds which we are now sowing at this place at this time. However, the Lord has demonstrated many times in the past that if even small deeds of men are in harmony with His will He may bless such deeds and cause a harvest which is far beyond our expectation or comprehension. We therefore would pray that the seeds which we are now planting will receive the blessing of God and that the fruit which may eventually come forth will be a delight to both man and his Maker.

For centuries the peoples of Europe have suffered the horrors of recurring war—needless conflicts perpetrated by irresponsible individuals who have sought to dominate not only the minds of the people of their own countries, but the peoples of neighboring nations as well. This lust for domination has usually resulted in armed conflicts—needless struggles in which all sides were the losers. The folly and insanity of such international conflicts were finally realized as a consequence of the ravages of the Second World War.

Since the termination of that War, most peoples of Europe including their leaders, have conscientiously set about the noble task of understanding and cooperating with their neighbors. To date, the extent and rewards of this friendly international understanding have been both revealing and amazing. There is now every indication that a new era for the peoples of Europe has been successfully launched.

Since World War II, literally scores of international organizations have been established. Most of these bodies have headquarters (of a temporary nature for the most part) which are located in one or another city of Western Europe.

Perhaps the most meaningful of the existing organizations deal with international economics. The vitality of the European Common Market is no longer questioned. There is every reason to believe that all of the countries of Western Europe will be united, economically, within a year, if not sooner.

If economic unity can be achieved, some form of political unity may not be far behind. With economic unity almost assured, and with political unity highly probable, there emerges the need for a recognizable focal point—a central area—a capital city—a physical symbol of a continent united.

We are gathered here today—the 8th day of September, 1961, to designate a site for such a capital city. This somewhat informal ceremony is, in a real sense, a "pre-dedication" of a site for that city. In commemoration of this occasion, we have now built an altar. We here this day call upon God to heed our prayer for a more lasting European peace—an era of good will toward all men—a period of freedom and justice, where the rights of all human beings, as individuals, are firmly established, and where all men and women as God-fearing creatures, may live free from political and religious tyranny.

If economic and political unity can be achieved, peace, freedom, and justice, with a truly representative form of government may logically be expected. These attributes can be the goals of the peoples of a united Europe, and these goals can be achieved if such is the will of the people.

We believe that this will, and the positive, unifying results which can be expected from the exercising of that will, can be symbolized in no more noble symbol than a new, beautiful city.

We propose that this new capital be located here in the heart of the Continent—here at the crossroads of the peoples of Europe. It is further suggested that a living body of water— a lake—be created at the heart of the city, and that the name of the capital of a United Europe be "Lake Europa."

A United Europe can be achieved—and in the near future.

We here today pray to Almighty God that the peoples of Europe may soon realize the blessings of political unity and the establishment of a new capital—the City of Lake Europa. May we here today—representing the old world and the new—join our resources, our minds, our hearts, our prayers, in common dedication to meet the challenges and opportunities which are now within our grasp. May the will of the people and the will of God be one. Amen.

BIBLIOGRAPHY

Bainton, Roland H. "Here I Stand." New York: Abingdon Press, 1950. 422 pp.

Ball, M. Margaret. "N.A.T.O. and the European Union Movement." New York: Frederick A. Praeger, 1959. 486 pp.

Blanshard, Paul. "The Irish and Catholic Power: An American Interpretation." Boston: The Beacon Press, 1953. 375 pp.

Bogardus, J. F. "Europe: A Geographical Survey." New York: Harper & Brothers, 1934. 713 pp.

Boyd, Andrew and Frances. "Western Union: A Study of the Trend Toward European Unity." Washington, D.C.: Public Affairs Press, 1949. 183 pp.

Bruun, Geoffrey. "Nineteenth Century European Civilization: 1815-1914." New York: Galaxy Book, Oxford University Press, 1960. 256 pp.

Cabot, Thomas D. "Common Market: Economic Foundation for a U. S. of Europe?" New York: Committee for Economic Development, 1959. 28 pp.

Carroll, J. M. "The Trail of Blood." Lexington (Kentucky): Ashland Avenue Baptist Church, 1931. 55 pp.

Committee for Economic Development. "The European Common Market & Its Meaning to the United States." New York: Committee for Economic Development, 1959. 152 pp.

Coudenhove-Kalergi, Count. "An Idea Conquers the World." London: Hutchinson & Company, 1953. 310 pp.

Coudenhove-Kalergi, Richard N. "Pan-Europe." New York: Alfred A. Knopf, 1926. 215 pp.

D'Aubigné, J. H. Merle. "The Life and Times of Martin Luther." Chicago: Moody Press, 1958. 559 pp.

Dewhurst, J. Frederick, John O. Coppock, P. Lamartine Yates, and Associates, "Europe's Needs and Resources." New York: The Twentieth Century Fund, 1961. 1198 pp.

"The Encyclopaedia Britannica" (Fourteenth Edition). London: The Encyclopaedia Britannica Company, Ltd., 1938. Vol. 12. 1005 pp.

"The Europa Year Book 1962." London: Europa Publications, Ltd., 1962. Vol. 1, 1262 pp.

"The European Economic Community: A Case Study of the New Economic Regionalism." In two parts. College Park (Maryland): Bureau of Economic Research, University of Maryland. Vol. 13, No. 2, September 1959. 16 pp., Vol. 13, No. 3, December 1959, 12 pp.

"European Yearbook," Vol. VII. Published under the auspices of the Council of Europe. The Hague: Martinus Nijhoff, 1960. 800 pp.

Evangelical Confederation of Colombia, "Bulletins." Published occasionally by the Office of Information and Public Relations of the Confederation, Headquarters in Barranquilla, Colombia.

Florinsky, Michael T. "Integrated Europe?" New York: The Macmillan Company, 1955. 182 pp.

Gibbon, Edward. "The Decline and Fall of the Roman Empire." Great Books of the Western World, Volumes 40 and 41. Chicago: Encyclopaedia Britannica, Inc., 1952. Vol. 1, 900 pp.; Vol. 2, 855 pp.

Goff, James E. "What's Behind the Persecution in Colombia?" "Latin America Evangelist." May-June 1961. pp. 2-5. (Published bi-monthly by the Latin America Mission, San Jose, Costa Rica.)

Hass, Ernst B. "The Uniting of Europe: Political, Social, and Economic Forces, 1950-1957." Stanford (California): Stanford University Press, 1958. 526 pp.

Heilbroner, Robert L. "Forging a United Europe: The Story of the European Community." Public Affairs Pamphlet No. 308. New York: Public Affairs Committee, Inc., 1961. 28 pp.

Huizinga, J. H. "Mr. Europe: A Political Biography of Paul Henri Spaak." New York: Frederick A. Praeger, 1961. 248 pp.

"International Organizations." Amsterdam: J. H. de Bussy, 1960. 99 pp.

Lea, Henry Charles. "A History of the Inquisition of the Middle Ages." New York: Russell & Russell, 1958. In three volumes. Vol. I, 583 pp.; Vol. II, 587 pp.; Vol. III, 736 pp.

Lindsay, Kenneth. "European Assemblies: The Experimental Period, 1949-1959." London: Stevens & Sons, Ltd., 1960. 267 pp.

Macmillan, Harold "Britain the Commonwealth and Europe." London: Conservative and Unionist Central Office. N.D. (issued 9 October 1962). 10 pp.

Matthews, Herbert L. "The Yoke and the Arrows: A Report on Spain." New York: George Braziller, Inc., 1957. 203 pp.

Nutting, Anthony. "Europe Will Not Wait: A Warning and a Way Out." New York: Frederick A. Praeger, 1960. 122 pp.

Pirenne, Henri. "A History of Europe." New York: University Books, 1955. 625 pp.

Porteous, David. "Calendar of the Reformation." New York: Loizeaux Brothers, 1960. 96 pp.

Robertson, A. H. "The Council of Europe: Its Structure, Functions and Achievements." Second Edition. New York: Frederick A. Praeger, 1961. 288 pp.

Robertson, A. H. "European Institutions: Cooperation-Integration-Unification. London: Stevens & Sons, Ltd., 1959. 372 pp.

Roeder, William S., Editor. "Dictionary of European History." New York: Philosophical Library, 1954. 316 pp.

Sennholz, Hans F. "How Can Europe Survive?" New York: D. Van Nostrand Company, 1955. 336 pp.

Shackleton, Margaret Reid. "Europe: A Regional Geography." London: Longmans, Green and Company, 1950. (Fourth Edition). 525 pp.

Shepherd, William R., "Atlas of Medieval and Modern History." New York: Holt and Company, 1932. 80 pp. maps plus 42 pp. index.

Smith, Howard K. "The State of Europe." New York: Alfred A. Knopf, 1949. 422 pp.

Sparks, John B. "The Histomap." Chicago: Rand McNally & Company, 1942 Edition. One Sheet.

Streit, Clarence K. "Union Now." New York: Harper & Brothers, 1938. 315 pp.

Taylor, Clyde W. "The Fate of Protestants in Colombia," "Christianity Today." (Published in Washington, D.C.). Vol. 11, No. 2, (October 28, 1957), pp. 11 - 13; and Vol. 11, No. 3, (November 11, 1957), pp. 15 - 17.

Von Schwarzenfeld, Gertrude. "Charles V, Father of Europe." Chicago: Henry Regnery Company, 1957. 307 pp.

Wells, H. G. "The Outline of History." Garden City (New York): Garden City Publishing Company, Inc., 1931. 1255 pp.

"Western Cooperation in Brief." London: Cox and Sharland, 1958. 39 pp. (Distributed by the British Information Services).

Woods, Henry M. "Our Priceless Heritage: A Study of Christian Doctrine in Contrast with Romanism." Harrisburg (Pennsylvania): The Evangelical Press, 1953. (Third Edition). 213 pp.

"Yearbook of International Organizations" 7th Edition, 1958-59. Brussels: Union of International Associations, 1958. 1269 pp.

Zurcher, Arnold J. "The Struggle to Unite Europe, 1940-1958." New York: New York University Press, 1958. 254 pp.

POSTSCRIPT

*Determine that the thing can and
shall be done, and then we shall
find the way.*
> *Abraham Lincoln*
> *1809-1865*

J. Marshall Miller

(Photo by G. D. Hackett)

Author; Lecturer; Former Planning Director of Pasadena, California; Organizer and director of seven studytours (three to Europe); Visiting Professor in Town Planning, Royal Academy of Fine Arts, Copenhagen, 1954-55; Guest lecturer on four lecture tours in Germany, 1955-57; Program Director, First International Seminar on Urban Renewal, held in The Hague, 1958; Editor, "New Life for Cities Around the World: International Handbook on Urban Renewal," 1959; Executive Director, Books International, publishers and distributors of significant material on urban development; Partner, Miller Associates, Planning Consultants, planners of Twin Parks, Ohio, America's first two interstate motorparks; Associate Professor of Planning, School of Architecture, Columbia University, New York City; Program Director, The Protestant Center, New York World's Fair, 1964-1965. Member, American Institute of Planners; American Society of Planning Officials; International Fraternity of Lambda Alpha (Land Economics); Inter-American Planning Society; German Academy for City and Regional Planning; President, Christian Music Association; etc.

44937